SERIES EDITOR: JOHN MOORE

ORDER OF BATTLE SERIES: 3

QUÉBEC
THE HEIGHTS OF ABRAHAM 1759
THE ARMIES OF WOLFE AND MONTCALM

RENÉ CHARTRAND

First published in Great Britain in 1999 by Osprey Publishing,
Elms Court, Chapel Way, Botley, Oxford OX2 9LP

ISBN 1 85532 847 X

Osprey Series Editor: Lee Johnson
Ravelin Series Editor: John Moore
Research Co-ordinator: Diane Moore
Design: Ravelin Limited, Braceborough, Lincolnshire, United Kingdom
Cartography: Chapman Bounford and Associates, London, United Kingdom

Origination by Valhaven Ltd, Isleworth, United Kingdom
Printed through Worldprint Ltd, Hong Kong

99 00 01 02 03   10 9 8 7 6 5 4 3 2 1

FOR A CATALOGUE OF ALL BOOKS PUBLISHED BY OSPREY MILITARY, AUTOMOTIVE AND AVIATION PLEASE WRITE TO:

The Marketing Manager, Osprey Publishing Ltd., P.O. Box 140, Wellingborough, Northants, NN8 4ZA United Kingdom

OR VISIT OUR WEBSITE AT:
http://www.osprey-publishing.co.uk

Series style

The style of presentation adopted in the Order of Battle series is designed to provide quickly the maximum information for the reader.

Order of Battle Unit Diagrams – All 'active' units in the ORBAT, that is those present and engaged on the battlefield are drawn in black. Those units not yet arrived or those present on the battlefield but unengaged are 'shadowed'.

Unit Data Panels – Similarly, those units which are present and engaged are provided with company details for infantry and cavalry bodies and with details of the pieces for artillery.

Battlefield Maps – Units engaged are shown in the respective colours of their armies. Units shown as 'shadowed' are those deployed for battle but not engaged at the time.

Order of Battle Timelines

Battle Page Timelines – Each volume concerns the Order of Battle for the armies involved. Rarely are the forces available to a commander committed into action as per his ORBAT. To help the reader follow the sequence of events, a Timeline is provided at the bottom of each 'battle' page. This Timeline gives the following information:

The top line bar defines the actual time of the actions being described in that battle section.

The middle line shows the time period covered by the whole day's action.

The bottom line indicates the page numbers of the other, often interlinked, actions covered in this book.

0800 hrs	0900	1000	1100	1200	1300	1400
pp45–47				50–51	52–55	

Publisher's note

Readers may wish to study this title in conjunction with the following Osprey publications:

MAA 48 *Wolfe's Army*
MAA 261 *18th Century Highlanders*
MAA 285 *King George's Army 1*
MAA 289 *King George's Army 2*
MAA 292 *King George's Army 3*
MAA 296 *Louis XV's Army 1 Cavalry*
MAA 302 *Louis XV's Army 2 French Infantry*
MAA 304 *Louis XV's Army 3 Foreign Infantry*
MAA 308 *Louis XV's Army 4 Light Troops*
MAA 314 *Louis XV's Army 5 Colonial & Naval Troops*

Key to Military Series symbols

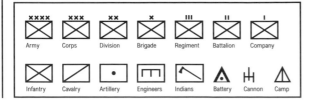

Author's acknowledgements

In the preparation of this volume, many people and institutions have been most helpful. Colonel Ian McCulloch generously shared the results of his research on the 1759 campaign. Colonel Jacques W. Ostiguy lent invaluable books and documents from his personal library. Pierre-Louis Lapointe of the Archives Nationales de Québec provided much documentary help. Peter Harrington of the Anne S.K. Brown Military Collection at Brown University kindly assisted with visual material, as did the Canadian War Museum and the National Archives of Canada. And last but not least, the editors John and Diane Moore. To one and all, please accept my heartfelt expression of deepest gratitude.

CONTENTS

STRATEGY IN NORTH AMERICA   **4**

THE DEFENCE OF QUÉBEC – Planning   **8**

THE ASSAULT ON QUÉBEC – Planning   **12**

MONTCALM'S COMMAND   **16**

The French Metropolitan Regiments   19

FRENCH COLONIAL TROOPS AND MILITIAS – Colonial Staff of New France   **26**

French Colonial Troops   28

French Colonial Militias   31

Corps of Cavalry, The Indians and La Marine   34

WOLFE'S COMMAND   **37**

1st Brigade   41

2nd Brigade   47

3rd Brigade   52

Royal Artillery, Louisbourg Grenadiers and Light Infantry   57

New England Rangers and Colonial Pioneers   60

THE ROYAL NAVY   **62**

PRELIMINARIES – Descent on Québec   65

The Siege of Québec   68

The Battle of Montmorency   70

Raids and Fighting Patrols   75

THE HEIGHTS OF ABRAHAM – Preparations   78

Amphibious Assault   81

THE HEIGHTS OF ABRAHAM – The Battle   **84**

Finale   92

WARGAMING QUÉBEC   **96**

SELECT BIBLIOGRAPHY   **96**

STRATEGY IN NORTH AMERICA

By the middle of the 18th century, New France formed an enormous arc right across North America. Yet its population was small at only about sixty to seventy thousand souls by the 1750s, the great majority settled along the St Lawrence River in Canada.

South and east of New France, along the Atlantic seaboard, British settlers flourished in a collection of several large colonies in what was increasingly known as 'New England'. The growth of these colonies was spectacular and the population stood at about a million and a half by the middle of the 18th century. Unlike the French colonies, who largely depended on the fur trade with the Indians, the economies of the British colonies were largely based on agriculture, commerce and fishing. In many ways, the English colonists sought to establish European-style communities which would take over the land for farms and plantations.

From the 1670s the French adopted an imperial global strategy regarding North America which evolved because of the explorations made into the interior of the continent. To them, the control of the waterways was crucial. Accordingly, forts with small detachments of regular colonial troops could be found on all the Great Lakes and down the Mississippi River by the early 18th century. These forts served as trading posts and as potential bases for raids against enemy Indians and New England. The Anglo-Americans were thus kept on the defensive at the edge of the forest. To secure the safety of the St Lawrence River, the fortress town and naval base of Louisbourg was built from the 1720s on Cape Breton Island.

The French in Canada – whose inhabitants became known as 'Canadians' – and their Indian allies dominated the forest while the sea was essentially controlled by the British. Louisbourg would prove to be the chink in the armour of New France.

In the early 1750s, the French moved into the Ohio Valley to secure this link with the Mississippi. Forts were built but fighting broke out with Virginians in 1754.

King George II of England.
(The National Portrait Gallery, London)

France and Britain sent metropolitan army troops to their respective colonies in unprecedented numbers during 1755.

The Seven Years' War broke out between Britain and France in September 1756 but did not produce much success for British arms. Even before war was declared, there had been Braddock's disastrous defeat in the Ohio Valley against Canadians and Indians and the repulse at Lake George of an attack by French metropolitan troops, led by Major-General Jean-Armand, Baron de Dieskau.

King Louis XV of France.
(Print after Quentin de La Tour's 1746 portrait)

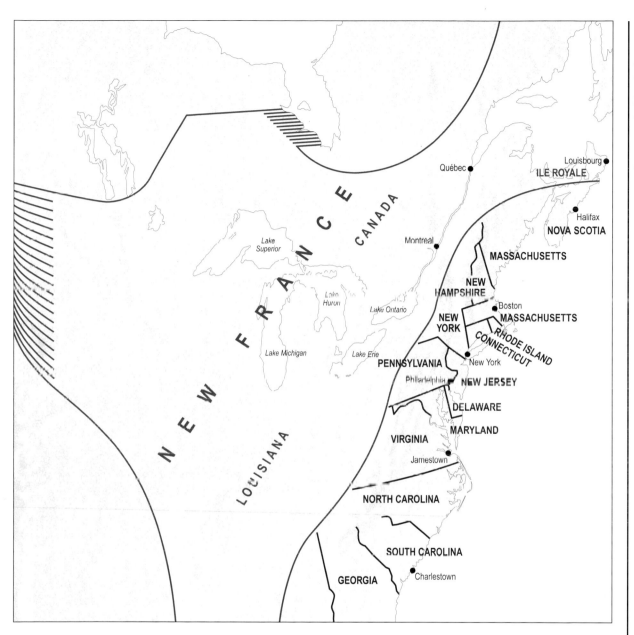

The vast crescent of New France, with the British colonies clustered along the eastern seaboard of North America.

Dieskau's replacement to command the French metropolitan troops arrived in May 1756 with two additional army battalions. He was Major-General Louis-Joseph, Marquis de Montcalm, a fiery character and prone to value only his own preconceived opinions, pretentious and sure of himself and full of terribly disparaging comments about colonial officers which he freely voiced without restraint or manners.

Born in 1712, Montcalm came from a noble family of Provence and had been in the army since age 12.

Seeking promotion and active command, he was appointed to Canada with the rank of maréchal de camp (major-general) although he had never held senior command. Energetic and a fine field commander, Montcalm captured forts Oswego and William-Henry in 1756 and 1757 and defeated General Abercromby at Carillon/Ticonderoga in 1758. Unfortunately, he could not resist negative comments about Governor-General Vaudreuil, his Canadian officers and the tactics they used. This attitude did nothing for cohesion amongst the small force of regulars.

The British too had their problems in their relations with colonial Americans. Regular officers were unsparing in their criticism of New Englanders which

Lord Loudoun, who briefly commanded the British forces in North America, was the general who developed the master strategy for the conquest of New France. (Print after portrait)

naturally created resentment among the American provincial troops. However, in the initial years of the war, the British regulars did not do very well against the French in North America. Whatever their differences, the French took the initiative and Montcalm captured Fort Oswego in 1756.

Such a setback to the theoretically stronger Anglo-Americans was largely due to the lack of a strategy to conquer New France. Major-General John Campbell, Earl of Loudoun was sent to America to command the British and colonial forces. A protégé of the Duke of Cumberland, Loudoun was a shrewd and experienced senior officer who had been ADC to the King. He soon recognised that the problem with the war in America was the absence of a comprehensive strategy. He therefore immediately went to work and, by early 1757, had formulated an ambitious strategic plan for the conquest of New France. It called for three simultaneous invasion routes by three armies.

The overall success of this concerted strategic plan depended on the doctrine of overwhelming force, mobilising up to 60,000 men from Britain and America, roughly the equivalent of the French population of Canada.

The strategy called for one Anglo-American army to attack up the Ohio Valley and Lake Ontario before heading east to Montréal.

Another Anglo-American army would go up Lake Champlain and the valley of the Richelieu River, approaching Montréal from the south. A further large army – almost all British regulars – with considerable Royal Naval support was to first capture Louisbourg to clear the entrance to the St Lawrence River, then sail up to Québec, besiege and take it. With the capital and main fortress in Canada taken, French resistance would be effectively smashed. The final step would be for the victorious Québec army to march west along the St Lawrence River to Montréal. All three armies would then close in on the city.

It was a truly grand strategy. Loudoun, like many men

on both sides of the Atlantic, believed that New France could only be vanquished by striking at its heart and taking the legendary fortress city of Québec. Thus, a vast expedition by sea would be required to take the place. It was the key to Loudoun's strategy. Once that was done, the meeting of the three armies at Montréal, and its final surrender, was a foregone conclusion. It was fortunate that William Pitt came to power in England from July 1757 and shifted Britain's main war effort from Europe to America. As Pitt gained more information about the state of affairs in North America, he became more convinced than ever that England's wealth and glory was to be found overseas. The war in Canada was therefore to be prosecuted with vigour and Pitt's ministry unleashed lavish expenditures to attain this objective. George II was initially reluctant to abandon Germany but reassured that a strong British

William Pitt, the British prime minister. (MARS)

force would also be present there, and with prospects of adding territories to his empire, the King endorsed the plan and supported it thereafter.

Although a superb planner, Loudoun was blamed for the loss of William-Henry to Montcalm and for the failure to mount an expedition to take Louisbourg although this was due to bad weather.

The underlying problem was that Pitt, for political reasons, had pressed for both Louisbourg and Québec to be taken the same year...! It was an impossibility but the ministry would not be denied. Late in 1757 Loudoun was recalled, primarily for political reasons and with his military reputation untarnished. He retained the respect of his officers. Colonel James Robertson neatly summing up Loudoun as having 'unblemished uprightness, unwearyed diligence, uncommon spirit and capacity joined to every amiable value ... when qualities like his bring disgrace, I shall not be overanxious for preferment.' Another remarked later that 'Amherst came *à propos* to reap the innumerable advantages from the labours of a Loudoun'.

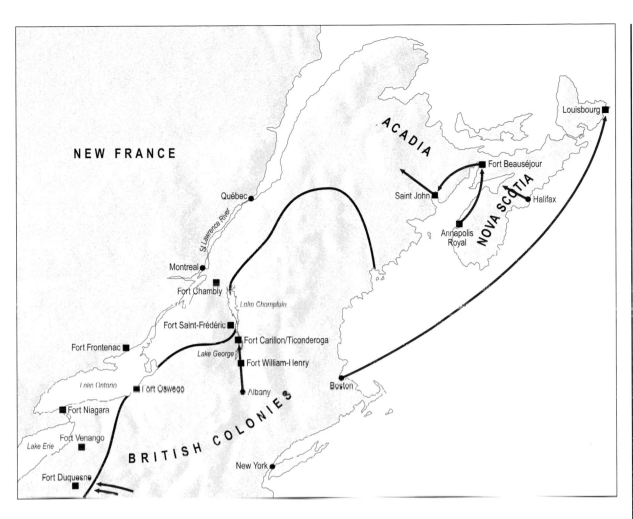

British military operations in North America, 1758 – the three-pronged attack on New France. The Ohio Valley fell to the British by the year's end but they were repulsed at Fort Carillon. Most important, the fall of Louisbourg opened the way to Québec.

Indeed, his strategy continued to be followed by his successors, almost to the letter. There was really no choice if Québec was to be taken. The steps laid out by Loudoun simply had to be followed. While the strategy was sound, the execution proved difficult for the Anglo-Americans. It was Pitt's misfortune that Loudoun's replacement as Commander in Chief in North America, Major-General James Abercromby, did not have the talents of his predecessor. In spite of a superiority in numbers, he proved a poor tactician compared to his opponent. Abercromby and his army suffered a terrible defeat at the hands of Montcalm and his French battalions at Ticonderoga on 8 July 1758. The Lake Champlain invasion route had failed again.

But in the Ohio, General Forbes' army eventually managed to force the French to evacuate their forts. Further east, the expedition against Louisbourg finally took place under Sir Jeffery Amherst. After a long and hard-fought siege, the French fortress surrendered on 26 July. On the British side, the bravery and tactical sense of a young brigadier had caught the eye at Louisbourg. His name was James Wolfe.

With Louisbourg taken, the St Lawrence and the route to Québec was now open, and the British forces could now, at last, attack the capital of New France. For this crucial 1759 campaign, overall command of the British forces in America was given to the cautious and methodical Lieutenant-General Sir Jeffery Amherst.

Following Loudoun's strategy, he would personally command the large Anglo-American army on the Lake Champlain front whose objectives would be forts Carillon, Saint-Frédéric and Montréal. Another strong Anglo-American force would come up from the south-west to attack the large French fort at Niagara guarding the western tip of Lake Ontario. Its capture would cut off French forts and settlements, such as Detroit, further west. The beginning of the end for New France would be in sight.

THE DEFENCE OF QUÉBEC

Planning

In all there were probably over 16,000 men under Montcalm's command for the defence of Québec, although some put the garrison at two or three thousand fewer. However numerous they may have been, they certainly were of variable quality. The most dependable were the regular soldiers, both metropolitan and colonial. Their elite were the grenadier companies, one to each of the five metropolitan battalions. The cavalry, the gunners, the Acadians and the more seasoned militiamen, experienced woodsmen and skirmishers, proved a match for anything thrown at them. Much of the remaining militia could only be used as firemen, depot guards and for transporting supplies. The Indians were practically a law unto themselves and, while very useful at times, could not be depended upon by Montcalm. They were allies but they were also doing some 'fence sitting' awaiting the outcome of the con-

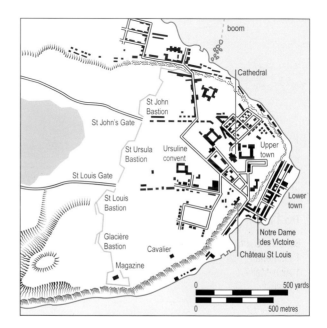

Above: **The defences of the city of Quebec. The Plains of Abraham are to the left, outside the city walls.**

Below: **View of Québec, 1700. Beauport is off to the right while the Plains of Abraham are to the left of the city.**
(British Museum, London)

COMPOSITION OF FRENCH LINE INFANTRY BATTALIONS

In all, a total establishment of 557 officers and men including 39 officers.

The following applies for the 2nd battalions of La Reine, Languedoc, Guyenne and Béarn sent to New France in 1755 and also to La Sarre and Royal-Roussillon sent in 1756. The battalion strength was ordered raised to 17 companies in France but this was not implemented in Canada.

However, a royal order of 25 February 1757 instructed that the establishment strength of the six battalions in Canada be raised as follows: each grenadier company to be increased from 45 to 50 NCOs and privates, each fusilier company to be increased from 40 to 50 NCOs and privates. However, this level of strength was probably never reached, or only for a short time.

Battalion Staff:
1 Lieutenant-Colonel   Officer Commanding
1 Aide-Major
1 Surgeon-Major

Grenadier Company (one per battalion):
1 Captain
1 Lieutenant
1 Sub-Lieutenant
2 Sergeants
2 Corporals
2 Anspsades (Lance Corporals)
1 Drummer
38 Grenadier Privates

Fusilier Company (12 companies per battalion):
1 Captain
1 Lieutenant
1 Sub-Lieutenant
2 Sergeants
2 Corporals
2 Anspsades (Lance Corporals)
1 Drummer
33 Fusilier Privates

COMPOSITION OF LE RÉGIMENT DE BERRY'S LINE INFANTRY BATTALIONS

The 2nd and 3rd battalions of Berry, sent to New France in 1757, had a different organisation with nine company battalions.

Battalion Staff:
1 Lieutenant-Colonel – Officer Commanding
1 Aide-Major
1 Ensign

Grenadier Company (one per battalion):
1 Captain
1 Lieutenant
1 Sub-Lieutenant
3 Sergeants
4 Corporals
4 Anspsades (Lance Corporals)
1 Drummer
48 Grenadier Privates

Fusilier Company (8 companies per battalion):
1 Captain
1 Lieutenant
1 Sub-Lieutenant
3 Sergeants
4 Corporals
4 Anspsades (Lance Corporals)
1 Drummer
48 Fusilier Privates

test. Nevertheless they retained considerable psychological value against the Anglo-Americans who feared them greatly.

Feeding these men put a heavy strain on the colony. Since the beginning of the war, there had been increasing food shortages in Canada, and bread and meat had been rationed for a number of years. As the siege went on, this was to become a more intractable problem as the supplies of flour from France began to run out. How far French troops on short rations were at a disadvantage to the well-fed British soldiers and sailors can only be surmised.

From June onwards a joint 'War Council' brought together senior officers from the colonial and the metropolitan military establishments. It was made up of Governor-General Vaudreuil, Lieutenant-General Montcalm, Major-General Lévis, Intendant Bigot, Lieutenant-Colonel de Montreuil acting as 'aide-major général' a sort of quartermaster-general, King's Lieutenant de Ramezay, who was in effect the governor of Québec City, Lieutenant-Colonel de Bernetz of Royal-Roussillon, Commandant Dumas of the colonial troops, Lieutenant-Colonel de Pontleroy as chief engineer and Artillery commandant Mercier. It seems to have been

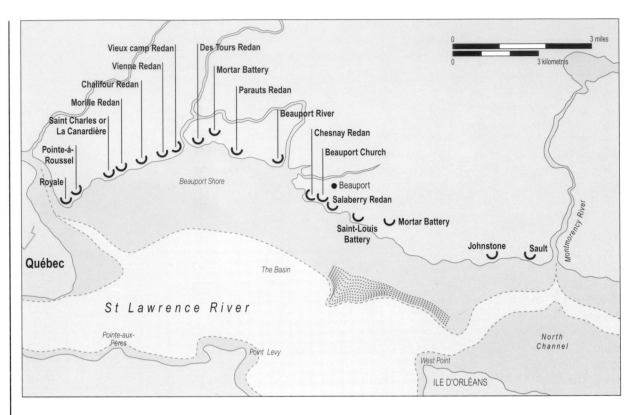

convened at the insistence of Vaudreuil as Montcalm commented that it was held to 'diminish the perplexities of M. de Vaudreuil' and obviously did not like it much.

The War Council structure is revealing in that it provided common ground on which the senior officers of Vaudreuil and Montcalm could meet. Each specialist service was organised under one officer. Engineering was headed by Chief Engineer de Pontleroy who was on the colonial establishment but had been in the army engineers previously and was thus liked by Montcalm. His subaltern engineers at Québec were from the army engineers. Artillery direction was assumed by the Chevalier Mercier, a career colonial gunner and thus constantly derided by Montcalm. About half of his regular artillery officers and part of his men were from the army's Royal-Artillerie.

Considerable energy was spent by thousands of men to build new fortifications and improve old ones all over the city. A strong barricade closed the Côte de la Montagne road to the upper city. The suburbs of St Roch and du Palais were enclosed and provided with 25 cannons. Some 66 cannons and seven mortars were installed between the Côte de la Montagne and the Potasse Bastion and another 52 cannon placed on the west side. Between the Château Saint-Louis and the Cape Diamond Redoubt, another two batteries holding 16 cannons and two mortars were built. But perhaps the most impressive effort was to fortify the length of the

Montcalm's fortified positions built on the Beauport shore in the spring of 1759. The defences were a myriad of redans and batteries, which successfully prevented Wolfe's troops from landing.

Beauport shore, from the falls of the Montmorency River, which would act as the eastern (or left) flank of the French army. Chief Engineer Pontleroy felt that it was

---

THE BEAUPORT LINES

Pointe-à-Roussel Battery, three 12-pounder cannons, flanked by two redans.
La Canardière Battery, three 12-pounders.
Morille Redan.
Chalifour Redan.
Vienne Redan.
Vieux camp Redan, three 8-pounders.
Des Tours Redan.
Parauts Redan, three 8-pounders.
Redoubt at the mouth of the Beauport River.
Chesnay Redan.
Salaberry Redan.
Redoubt below the church with two batteries, four 12-pounders.
Saint-Louis Battery with two redans to be built.
Sault Redoubt, three 8-pounders.

the weak spot, especially in the area about La Canardière where Phips' men had landed in 1690. A first entrenchment line was built in May running along the St Charles River up to the General Hospital. Pontleroy wanted to close access to the river and had two ships scuttled at its entrance. They were transformed into advanced batteries. Behind were more obstacles including a boat bridge and a floating battery called La Diable (The She-Devil) holding 18 24-pounder cannons. By the end of June, many redoubts and redans had been built along the Beauport shore, both on the cliff and on the beach, some mounted with guns.

The Sault Redoubt was the most easterly on the beach, just below the majestic-looking Montmorency Falls. Another work, the Johnstone Battery, was also built on the beach, about 900 metres west of the Sault Redoubt.

The great majority of the French troops, at least 12,000 men, were posted to defend the Beauport shore. The right wing of the defences, which began at the St Charles River and ran east, was under the command of Governor-General Vaudreuil and included some 3,000 Québec militiamen and 1,100 Trois-Rivières militia. The centre, considered the most vulnerable to a

A navy cannon on a garrison/naval carriage, from the first half of the 18th century. Older guns were generally mounted in coastal forts and the great majority of French cannons at Québec were of this type.
(Print from Saint-Rémy's Mémoires d'Artillerie)

landing, was under Montcalm and included the metropolitan battalions of La Sarre, Languedoc, Béarn and Royal-Roussillon in the first line and Guyenne in reserve to defend La Canardière and the village of Beauport. The left wing was under General Lévis and ran from east of the village of Beauport to the Montmorency Falls and river. It was manned by about 3,200 Montréal militiamen with about 600 soldiers of the colonial troops. Also lurking on the left wing were some 1,000 Indians with some Canadian woodsmen under the command of a famous colonial officer from Michilimackinac, Charles de Langlade, the son of a French officer and an Indian princess.

The Île d'Orléans was indefensible and would be abandoned as would the south shore. One possible 'mistake' made by the French generals was to leave Point Levy vulnerable. Many have said that a large and strong citadel like redoubt could have been built there by the French; that such a work might have denied access to the upper river to the British ships and would have prevented the British from installing batteries there. On the other hand, citadels, even of earth and timber, are not built overnight. Such a work would have required many men to garrison it. It could just as easily have been subjected to a hopeless siege, and cut off from the main French forces on the north bank. With limited supplies and few regular troops, it was not feasible and the notion was not seriously entertained by the French general staff. According to extracts of discussions during their meetings in Montcalm's journal they instead concentrated on defending the north shore .

As far as possible Montcalm and his officers had sought to keep their forces concentrated to defend the Beauport shore as the first priority. This was the place where Phips had landed troops in 1690, and they suspected the future British attackers would attempt to emulate this achievement. They were reasonably confident about the new fortifications built there.

There was no such confidence regarding the fortifications of the city itself. Bougainville believed that it was badly fortified but he was still a young officer with limited experience. However, the Sieur de Courville also felt the fortifications to be in very bad repair and noted that the gates were so defective that they could not be closed. More seriously, Montcalm also felt the same way. He wrote that 'the fortifications were so ridiculous and so bad that [the city] would be taken as it would be under siege'. This was something of an exaggeration but such views from a commanding general who had experienced siege warfare in Europe demonstrate serious concern. These concerns obviously influenced Montcalm's decision to march out to meet Wolfe on that fateful September day.

THE ASSAULT ON QUÉBEC

Planning

The embryo 'fort' at what was to become the city of Québec was begun on 3 July 1608 when Samuel de Champlain, with a party of French traders, started the construction of the first 'Habitation' at the foot of Cape Diamond. The small post flourished. In 1624, a larger habitation with castle-like stone turrets was built. In 1626, work started on Fort St Louis on top of Cape Diamond which, in time, became the Château St Louis, the residence of the governors of New France. While still an outpost, Québec was taken without a fight by English corsairs, the brothers Lewis and David Kirke in 1629. However, New France was returned to France by treaty and, in 1632, Québec was again under the French flag.

The city of Québec remained safe and its fortifications were slowly improved. Following Phips' unsuccessful attack, the 1690 line of bastioned earthworks was reinforced in 1693 and included the redoubt on top of Cape Diamond while, from 1691, a strong bastion-shaped battery, the Royal Battery, had been built to cover the docks area in the lower town. These works were joined by a couple of stone bastions and construction began on a new line of fortifications in the 1710s and 1720s but it remained unfinished.

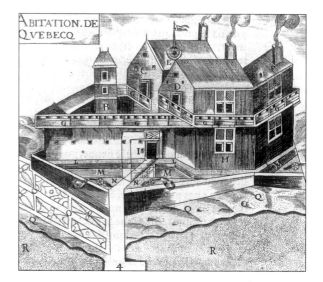

Above: The 'Habitation' was the first fort built by the French at Québec during 1608.
(National Library of Canada, L8769)

Below: The Comte de Frontenac replies 'by his cannon's mouth' to Sir William Phips' demand to surrender the city. (MARS)

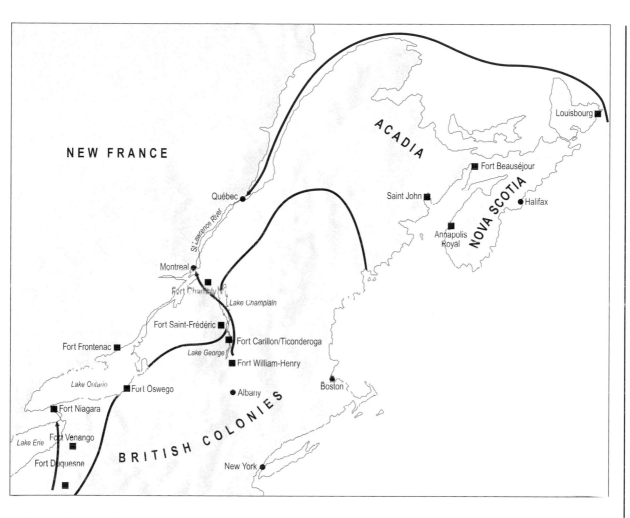

Thus, when the War of Austrian Succession broke out, chief King's Engineer Gaspard Chaussegros de Léry reported the city essentially unfortified on the landward side. A new line, its walls and bastions covered with stone revetments, was started in 1745 and completed in 1749. This major work resulted in essentially the walls of Québec as seen today. Older batteries were improved and new ones added in various parts of the city. As a result when hostilities resumed in 1756, the city had an extensive system of fortifications to complement its truly formidable natural defences.

Brigadier-General James Wolfe's assault on Québec was to be part of a three-pronged assault on New France. Wolfe would attack down the St Lawrence while the overall commander of British forces in north America, General Jeffery Amherst, would march with 12,000 men against Montréal via Ticonderoga and Crown Point. A third force, under Brigadier Prideaux, would assault Fort Niagara and then press on to Montréal to link up with Amherst and, eventually, with Wolfe.

It is clear at a glance that a number of important factors were overlooked in the planning and execution

Above: Following Loudoun's plan, Amherst was to attack along Lake Champlain, Prideaux was to advance via Fort Niagara while Wolfe moved to take Québec.

Right: **Sir Jeffery Amherst, General-in-Chief of the British forces in North America.** (Print after Sir Joshua Reynolds)

of this campaign. The timing for any sort expedition against Québec was, perhaps, the most crucial factor. The ice-free season was limited. Then there was the St Lawrence River itself, a difficult place to sail without good pilots and sounders. Finally, a site such as Québec – a natural fortress – required a major siege with considerable resources in men and equipment.

Wolfe recognised that he needed accurate information in order to gauge the magnitude of the task which faced him. The chief engineer he selected for the expedition, Patrick Mackellar, proved especially useful. He had been captured at Oswego by Montcalm's army in 1756 and had spent time as a prisoner in Québec. Following his release in 1757, he made a very detailed report on the fortifications of Québec for the Board of Ordnance in London. The report was made available to Wolfe. Mackellar felt the city to be poorly fortified but situated on a formidable site. His views largely concurred with a 1752 inspection made by French metropolitan engineer Franquet who felt the place to be impregnable even without elaborate fortifications. Mackellar's report included a plan based on one published in 1744 as part of Father Charlevoix's history of New France and stated he had not heard of further modifications being made since then. Thus he did not show the new line of walls on the west side of the city which had been built since 1745. Apart from Mackellar's report, there was little else available to Wolfe and his senior officers besides the French cartographer Bellin's maps and charts which gave no new information.

Even Thomas Jefferys' 'Authentic Plan' published after the 1759 siege showed the pre-1745 line of walls which gives an idea of the British 'intelligence gap' with regard to Québec. In the event, the whole issue of the fortifications west of the city was to be largely irrelevant. The first time Wolfe and his men were to see them was on 13 September in the distance, beyond Montcalm's army.

Information about Québec's surrounding area was also quite sketchy. The most promising area for a landing appeared to be the Beauport shore in the area of La Canadière, where the Massachusetts volunteers had landed in 1690. From all accounts available to Wolfe it was not fortified and therefore could apparently be occupied by a strong force of his regulars.

Wolfe spent the spring gathering what intelligence he could, chose his officers, and planned the expedition and its opening moves against the French once it was within sight of Québec. With all the information and advice he could gather, Wolfe felt that he would have to occupy the south shore of the St Lawrence near the city and especially Point Levy. It was a fine vantage point which commanded the narrows of the river. From its high bluffs, powerful batteries could bombard the city with considerable effect. As Wolfe put it to Amherst in March: 'I propose to set the Town on fire with Shells, to destroy the Harvest, Houses, & Cattle, both above & below [Québec], to send off as many Canadians as possible to Europe, & to leave famine and desolation behind me'.

The Beauport shore as far as the St Charles River would also have to be occupied by strong forces. His army could then be assembled east of the St Charles

---

BRITISH ARMY REGIMENTAL STRENGTH

In the British army, each battalion was made up of ten companies: nine of fusiliers or 'hat' men since they wore tricorn hats, and one of grenadiers which were the best and bravest soldiers in the unit who were distinguished by tall and ornate pointed caps. Most regiments had only one battalion but some, such as the 60th (Royal Americans) might have several. The number of officers and men within a regiment varied as the establishments voted by Parliament, which provided the money to pay the army, might differ from one regiment to another. And from one year to the next, since appropriations were voted yearly.

A standard rule of thumb has been to state that, in times of war, a British regiment of one battalion was 1000 men, divided into 100 men companies. In fact, the way to have a better idea of a battalion is to take its number of officers and men and divide it by ten. Thus at Québec, there were fewer than 600 in Amherst's 15th and Bragg's 28th, nearly 900 in Otway's 35th and over 1,200 in Fraser's 78th. Similarily, company strength could vary. The Louisbourg Grenadiers' companies had from 108 to 110 men, over the usual strength.

Also, to cope with conditions of warfare in North America, a temporary light infantry company was formed in each battalion to act as skirmishers. The uniforms of these men were cut down and they wore caps. It is not always clear if this was a temporary 11th company or one of the fusilier companies transformed for the occasion. It was, however, deemed very good since, after being disbanded when Montréal surrendered, a light infantry company was instituted permanently in each battalion from 1771.

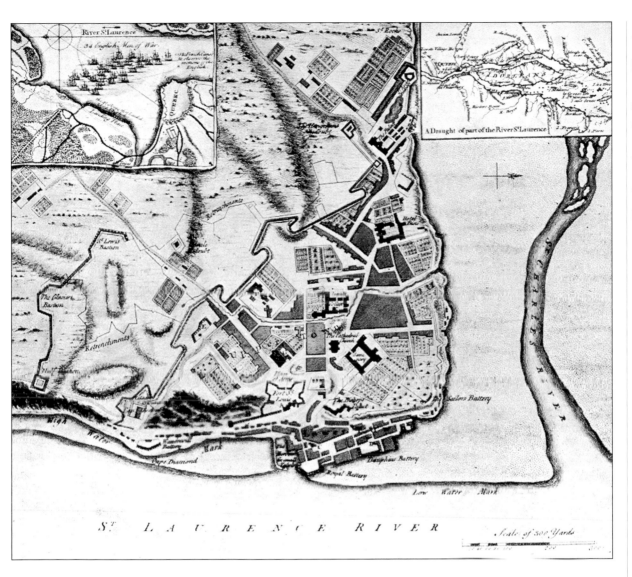

Map based on Major Patrick Mackellar's plan of the fortifications of the city of Québec.
(From a coloured plan oublished by E. Oakley, 1759)

River. His first choice for the attack on Québec was a general assault to carry the French positions on the far side of the St Charles River. This would be followed by an assault on the city itself.

This relied on the Beauport shore being unfortified or with only a few weak works that could be easily swept away. The reality that was to face Wolfe was very different. What seems to have been his main objective before he reached Québec, a landing at La Canardière, would prove impossible. An alternative would be to land further east near the Montmorency River and try to draw out Montcalm's army.

Finally he could land a strong force three to five miles above Québec that could entrench before the French attacked. Having secured this 'beachhead', the rest of the army would follow and attack the city on the west side. It has been suggested on the basis of this remark that from the beginning Wolfe planned to land at the Plains of Abraham. But at this stage he was simply considering a wide range of possible methods to attack the city. In any event Wolfe relied on the navy to secure the river below and above the city.

Naturally, Wolfe wondered in what sorts of spirits he would find the French defenders. In May, he noted that if 'I find that the enemy is strong, audacious, and well commanded, I shall proceed with the utmost caution and circumspection, giving Mr. Amherst time to use his superiority. If they are timid, weak, and ignorant, we shall push them with more vivacity' and take the city, then go to assist Amherst's army 'before the summer is gone'.

All these theories had yet to be put to the test.

15

MONTCALM'S COMMAND

What exactly Montcalm commanded had been the subject of fierce debate since 1756. He was supposed to have direct command of the metropolitan army battalions in Canada. According to the royal instructions from Louis XV, Governor-General Vaudreuil was to decide on the strategic aims of the campaigns with Montcalm determining tactics. They were to act in cooperation but the instructions were quite clear in that Vaudreuil would be the supreme authority. To complicate matters, colonial troops reported directly to Vaudreuil. This may have reflected the correct protocol but, in practice, putting an experienced soldier under the orders of a colonial governor whose military experience was likely to ruffle feathers. Each bickered about the other to his respective minister, Montcalm to the minister of War and

*Lieutenant-General Louis-Joseph,
Marquis de Montcalm*
Officer Commanding

*Major-General François Gaston,
Chevalier de Lévis*
2nd-in-Command and
ADC to General Montcalm

Colonel Louis Antoine de Bougainville
Acting Brigadier-General and
ADC to General Montcalm

Lieutenant-Colonel de Sennezergue
Acting Brigadier-General and
2nd-in-Command during General Lévis's absence
(August-September)

Jean-Guillaume de Plantavit
Chief-of-Staff to General Lévis

Chevalier de Johnstone
ADC to General Lévis and ADC to General Montcalm
(August–September)

Nicholas de Sarrebource de Pontleroy
Chief Engineer

Benoît-Françoise Bernier
Commissaires des Guerres

Vaudreuil to the minister of the Navy. As time passed this tension spread to their staff officers and, to a certain extent, to the officers of the metropolitan and colonial units. The animosity between the two factions hampered staff work and the coordination of planning.

Just before the siege of Québec a despatch was received from France detailing adjustments to the command structure which it was hoped would end the ongoing feud. In late 1758, an exasperated Montcalm

**Lieutenant-General Louis-Joseph,
Marquis de Montcalm.**
(National Archives of Canada C528)

MONTCALM'S COMMAND

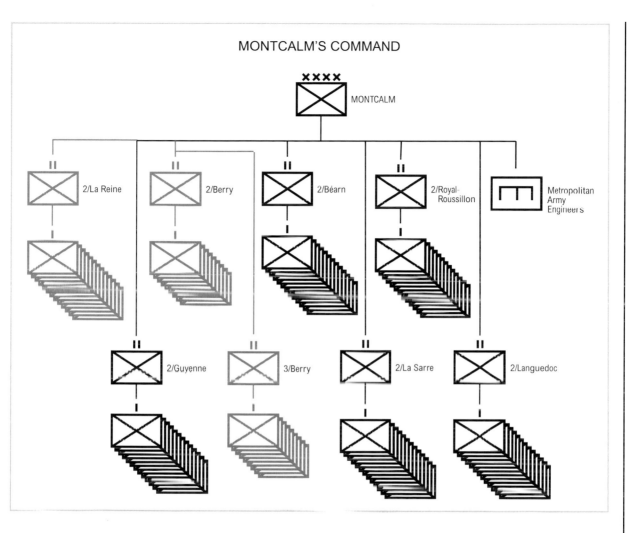

Major-General François-Gaston, Chevalier de Lévis, General Montcalm's Second in Command.

submitted his resignation to the minister of War and asked to be recalled to France. The French Court refused, recalling neither Montcalm nor Vaudreuil. Instead they instructed Vaudreuil that, on all military matters, he was to defer to Montcalm who was promoted to Lieutenant-General. But Vaudreuil, the Court went on, remained commander-in-chief and the supreme authority in the colony on all administrative, diplomatic and political matters. This was hardly a practical solution on the eve of a major siege and, in practice, command arrangements remained effectively unchanged. The bitterness remained and the feuding went on, but now Montcalm officially had the upper hand in purely military matters.

Fortunately, Montcalm's second in command was Major-General François-Gaston, Chevalier de Lévis, a pragmatic soldier who managed to keep on good terms with both Montcalm and Vaudreuil. In his capacity as second in command of the metropolitan troops in Canada, he handled military matters with great efficiency always a dependable and 'problem solving' sort of officer and much appreciated by the men. It was, however, his diplomatic skills and calm, firm yet objective approach which may have proven most valuable between 1756 and 1759. Like Montcalm, he clearly perceived the abuses in the colonial administration. But he recognised that in colonial eyes the metropolitan troops also had their faults. It seemed obvious to Lévis that little would be achieved through confrontation and animosity. Conciliation and

Louis-Antoine de Bougainville.
(Print after a portrait painted in later life)

France and was put in charge of a corps west of the city. His second, Captain de La Roche-Beaucourt, was from the Montcalm Cavalry Regiment and thus the perfect candidate to form the new Corps of Cavalry. This only left Captain Marcel as ADC to Montcalm so Royal-Artillerie Captain de Montbeillard became ADC. For his part, Major-General Lévis appointed as his ADC Captain the Chevalier James Johnstone, a Scottish Jacobite who had fled Scotland following the 1745 rebellion. Johnstone was commissioned in the colonial troops and proved most useful because of his perfect knowledge of English and French. He translated key dispatches and interrogated British prisoners and deserters.

The regular troops available to defend Canada consisted of only eight metropolitan battalions and the colonial troops with a handful of gunners, all under strength. The militia was excellent but getting weary. After 1757, no further troops were sent to reinforce Canada. Bougainville was sent to France to ask for reinforcements but the Minister of the Navy, Berryer, referring to France's defeats in Europe, replied that 'when the house was on fire, one did not bother with the stables.' As if all that was not bad enough, Bougainville returned bearing news that French spies had learned that a General 'Wolf' had left England with some 8,000 men intended for an expedition against Québec.

understanding were more likely to achieve positive results. What he saw as most vital was that the French command in Canada remain united against the overwhelming odds it had to face. Between 1756 and Montcalm's death, Lévis' influence and example no doubt soothed the feelings of many officers in both factions. It would have been of great benefit to New France if Montcalm had possessed the same diplomatic qualities.

Montcalm made changes to his own staff. His first ADC, de Bougainville, had been promoted to Colonel in

Montcalm was so concerned about a British landing on the Beauport shore that, in addition to batteries and redans, a complete system of entrenchments was built.

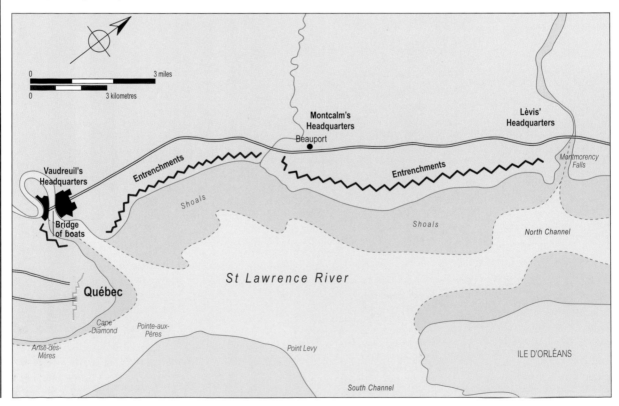

2ème Bataillon
LE RÉGIMENT DE LA REINE

The La Reine Regiment was raised on 3 October 1634. It was originally named after its first commander, Marshal d'Huxelles. The unit's name was changed to La Reine (The Queen's) on 12 March 1661 after the queen of France became the regiment's colonel-in-chief. While it was not a regiment of the royal guards, it was one of the few line infantry regiments to have a member of the royal family as its colonel. It had a long and distinguished record.

During the Seven Years' War, the 1st battalion of La Reine provided the garrison of several fortresses and saw no action until 1760 at Clostercamp subsequently serving in Germany until 1762.

> 1755: 32 Officers
>   525 NCOs and Men
> May 1759: 440
>
> 12 Fusilier Companies
> 1 Grenadier Company
> Uniform: grey-white coat, lining and breeches, red cuffs (three buttons) and collar, blue waistcoat, pewter buttons, silver hat lace, horizontal pocket with four buttons on each side
> Silver buttons for officers.

Private, La Reine Regiment, c. 1757-1760.
(Musée de l'Armée, Paris)

> ### 2nd BATTALION, LA REINE REGIMENT
> *Lieutenant-Colonel de Roquemaure*

In April 1755, La Reine's 2nd battalion, consisting of 32 officers and 525 men, in 12 fusilier and one grenadier company, embarked at Brest for New France. On the way, the French warship *Lis*, with four companies of La Reine and four companies from the 2nd Languedoc battalion on board, was captured by Admiral Boscawen's British fleet despite the fact that France and Britain had not officially declared war. However, most of the French fleet escaped and the remaining nine companies landed at Québec on 19 June.

Deployed to Fort St Frédéric on Lake Champlain, it was unlucky in its first action when it formed part of General Dieskau's force repulsed at Lake George on 8 September by Sir William Johnson's New England provincial militiamen. In August 1756, it participated in Montcalm's capture of Fort Oswego and the following August in the capture of Fort William-Henry. Four companies, replacing those lost on the *Lis*, joined the battalion in September 1757. It was present at the defeat of Abercromby's Anglo-American army at Ticonderoga in July 1758.

Although the battalion was part of Montcalm's command in Canada from 1756, it was not part of the forces defending Québec during the siege. Many have assumed it was present because one of the best known versions of a famous dialogue with a French sentry mentions a French-speaking British officer who answers 'La Reine' when challenged.

It did take up winter quarters in the Québec area but, during early May 1759, the battalion was sent to Fort Carillon south of Lake Champlain to protect against an attack from Britain's New England colonies. It remained as part of the garrison until the end of July when the fort was blown up by the French at the approach of General Amherst's much superior force. La Reine then retired and entrenched at Ile-aux-Noix, south of Montréal.

There were some La Reine personnel in Québec in 1759 as four officers and some recruits for the regiment landed there from France on 13 May.

2ème Bataillon

LE RÉGIMENT DE GUYENNE

R aised on 21 February 1684, the regiment was named after the province of Guyenne. During the Seven Years' War, the 1st battalion was on garrison duties on the Atlantic coast of France and saw no action.

In April 1755, the 2nd battalion embarked at Brest for New France and arrived at Québec on 23 June. In July, the battalion was sent west to garrison Fort Frontenac (now Kingston, Ontario) where it arrived on 10 August. In October, it was sent further west to Fort Niagara. Four companies were left there in garrison over the winter while the rest of the battalion went back to Montréal in November and wintered there.

> ### 2nd BATTALION, GUYENNE REGIMENT
> *Lieutenant-Colonel de Fontbonne*

In February 1756, a 19-man detachment took part in the attack on the British lines of communication behind Oswego and Lake George which resulted in the capture of Fort Bull. In June, the bulk of Guyenne at Montréal was reunited with the four companies at Fort Niagara. On 5 August, Guyenne joined General Montcalm together with the battalions of Béarn and La Sarre as well as artillery, colonial troops, militias and Indians for the siege of Fort Oswego between 10 and 14 August, when the Anglo-Americans surrendered. In the autumn, Guyenne was sent to Fort Carillon (Ticonderoga) and then took up its winter quarters at Québec, a detachment being sent to Fort Niagara. In May 1757, the regiment was sent to Fort Chambly and then, in July, back to Fort Carillon. Some 492 men from the battalion participated in the siege and capture of Fort William-Henry between 4 and 9 August 1757. In September, Guyenne again moved to the Chambly area were it took up winter quarters.

In June 1758, the battalion returned to Ticonderoga with other troops under Montcalm's command and, on 8 July, was posted on the right of the French line with La Reine and Béarn and participated in the defeat of Abercromby's invading Anglo-American army. The unit, with 393 men fit for service in August, remained at Ticonderoga until it went into winter quarters in the Chambly and Sorel areas.

In March 1759, a detachment of about 35 men was sent to Fort Niagara while another detachment of 30

1755: 31 Officers
        525 NCOs and Men
May 1759: 436

12 Fusilier Companies
1 Grenadier Company
Uniform: grey-white coat, lining and breeches, red cuffs (three buttons), collar and waistcoat, brass buttons, gold hat lace.
Gold buttons for officers.

Private, Guyenne Regiment, c. 1757-1760.
(Musée de l'Armée, Paris)

moved to Ile-aux-Noix two months later.

The rest of the battalion arrived at Québec in late May and participated in its defence. It took part in the battle of Montmorency on 31 July. During the defence of the Beauport Lines the battalion was held in reserve to defend La Canardière and Montcalm's headquaters at Beauport village.

On 13 September the battalion, along with Béarn, was deployed by Montcalm in the centre of his line at the start of the battle of the Plains. Following the action, two officers and 37 men from the unit who remained in the city surrendered on 18 September. The rest of the battalion retreated to Montréal.

On 10 December 1762, the Guyenne Regiment was incorporated into the Dauphin Regiment.

2ème & 3ème Bataillons
LE RÉGIMENT DE BERRY

The Berry Regiment was raised 2 September 1684 and bore the name of a French province. During the Seven Years' War, the 1st battalion was in garrison on the Atlantic coast of France and saw no action.

At the beginning of the war, the newly-raised 2nd and 3rd battalions of the regiment were originally intended to go to India. As a result, each battalion had nine companies including one of grenadiers instead of the standard 13 companies per battalion. However, there was a change in plans and, following Montcalm and Vaudreuil's pleas for more troops, Berry's destination was changed. The 18 companies embarked for Canada at Brest in April 1757, landing at Québec at the end of July.

> ### 2nd BATTALION, BERRY REGIMENT
> *Lieutenant-Colonel de Trivio*

Both battalions remained in the Québec area quartering at Beauport and on the Ile d'Orléans. In June 1758, the battalions moved to Fort Carillon, south of Lake Champlain, with the rest of Montcalm's land forces. On 8 July 1758, Berry took part in Montcalm's victory over the Anglo-Americans. The 2nd battalion was in the centre of the French position while the 3rd was defending the fort itself. By late August, the strength of both battalions had dwindled to 723 men fit for service. By November, the battalions were back at Beauport and the Ile d'Orléans where they wintered.

> ### 3rd BATTALION, BERRY REGIMENT
> *Lieutenant-Colonel de Trécesson*

Although part of Montcalm's command, the two battalions of the Berry Regiment were not to remain in Québec. In May 1759, both battalions were posted to Fort Carillon. It must have been with regret that Montcalm sent his most numerous regiment to Lake Champlain but Canada was also threatened from the south. They remained there until the end of July when the fort was blown up as General Amherst's much superior army approached. Berry moved north in August and entrenched itself in a strong position at Isle-aux-Noix, just north of Lake Champlain on the Richelieu River. Similarly to the La Reine Regiment, there were, however, some personnel from Berry at Québec in 1759

> 1755: 1,118 all ranks
> May 1759: 908
>
> 16 Fusilier Companies
> 2 Grenadier Companies
> Uniform: grey-white coat, lining and breeches, red collar, cuffs (five buttons) and waistcoat, brass buttons, gold hat lace, double vertical pockets.
> Gold buttons for officers.

as three officers and some recruits for the regiment arrived there from France in the middle of May.

After the fall of New France, the remnants of the two battalions from Canada were joined to the 1st battalion. Finally, as part of the vast reorganisation in the French army towards the end of the war, the Berry Regiment was incorporated into the Aquitaine Regiment on 10 December 1762.

Private, Berry Regiment, c. 1757-1760.
(Musée de l'Armée, Paris)

2ème Bataillon
LE RÉGIMENT DE BÉARN

The Béarn Regiment, named after the southern French province, was raised from 3 September 1684. During the Seven Years War, the 1st battalion was in garrison on the Atlantic coast of France and saw no action.

In April 1755 the 2nd battalion embarked at Brest for Canada as part of General Dieskau's force. It arrived safely and landed at Québec in June. It did not remain there for long. On 19 July, the battalion was sent to Fort Frontenac on Lake Ontario (now Kingston, Ontario) where it remained until December. In early June 1756, Béarn went on to Fort Niagara at the western end of Lake Ontario. It remained in garrison there until late July when it joined La Sarre, Guyenne, artillery, Canadian militiamen and Indians, all part of Montcalm's army that gathered to attack the British at Oswego. The British surrendered after a four day siege on 14 August.

> **2nd BATTALION, BÉARN REGIMENT**
> *Lieutenant-Colonel d'Alquier*

The Béarn battalion then moved to Montréal and was quartered south of the city. During the winter, a small detachment took part in the capture of Fort Bull on the

1755: 31 Officers
525 NCOs and Men
May 1759: 454

12 Fusilier Companies
1 Grenadier Company
Uniform: grey-white coat, lining and breeches, red collar, cuffs (three buttons) and waistcoat, brass buttons, gold hat lace, double vertical pockets.
Gold buttons for officers.

Private, Béarn Regiment, c. 1757-1760.

(Musée de l'Armée, Paris)

Mowhawk River portage, where the British lost 60 killed and all their horses before the powder magazine was blown up. Another detachment from the battalion raided Fort William-Henry. In May the following year the unit was sent to Fort Carillon and, in August, Béarn's 464 men joined the rest of Montcalm's army which commenced the siege of Fort William-Henry on 4 August. The fort fell to the French five days later.

The battalion then returned to Fort Carillon where it remained until it again took up winter quarters in Montréal. In June 1758, Béarn was back at Ticonderoga with the rest of Montcalm's forces. On 8 July, the battalion contributed to the defeat of Abercromby's Anglo-American army. It was posted on the right of the French line with La Reine and Guyenne. By August, it had 393 men fit for duty.

After wintering yet again in the Montréal area, a detachment of about 35 men was sent to Fort Niagara in June 1759. The rest of the battalion participated in the defence of Québec. Béarn was deployed in the first line at the centre of the Beauport Lines and was instrumental in repulsing the attempted British landings at the battle of Montmorency on 31 July.

On the morning of 13 September the battalion, along with Guyenne, was deployed by Montcalm in the centre of his line. A detachment of two officers and 31 men in the city surrendered on 18 September. The remainder of the battalion had retreated to Montréal.

On 25 November 1762 the Béarn Regiment was disbanded as a result of general reorganisation of the French army.

2ème Bataillon
LE RÉGIMENT DE LA SARRE

This Regiment was raised on 20 May 1651 as La Ferté's, after the name of its first colonel, the Duc de la Ferté. In 1685 the Regiment took the name of La Sarre. During the Seven Years' War, the 1st battalion was on garrison at La Rochelle on the Atlantic coast of France and saw no action until 1762 when this battalion was sent to Portugal via Spain. It took part in the siege of Almeida and was back in France by 1763.

The 2nd battalion embarked in March 1756 at Brest on a fleet bound for Canada and arrived at Québec on 3 June. It was sent first to Montréal and then to Niaroué Bay (Sacketts Harbor, NY), where it joined Montcalm and the Béarn and Guyenne regiments with artillery, militiamen and Indians. The battalion took part in the siege and capture of Fort Oswego from 10 to 14 August. It later escorted the British prisoners (50th and 51st Foot, New Jersey Provincial Regiment) back to Montréal. Its winter quarters were in the outlying area of Montréal.

> ## 2nd BATTALION, LA SARRE REGIMENT
> *Lieutenant-Colonel de Sennezergues*

During the winter, small parties from La Sarre took part in the successful capture of Fort Bull and a raid on Fort William-Henry. In May 1757, the battalion was sent to Fort Carillon. In August, 451 men from the unit were with Montcalm's army which besieged Fort William-Henry. After a winter spent at Ile Jésus north of Montréal, La Sarre returned to Fort Carillon where it was part of Montcalm's force which defeated General Abercromby's Anglo-American army on 8 July 1758. La Sarre held the left of the French line with Languedoc. By the end of August, it had 436 men fit for service. In 1759, after a winter spent in the Montréal area, a detachment of about 35 men was sent to Fort Niagara, while the rest of the battalion participated in the defence of Québec. It took part in the battle of Montmorency on 31 July.

The battalion was marched from the Beauport Lines to the Plains of Abraham early on the morning of 13 September. La Sarre was deployed on the right of Montcalm's centre, along with the other Metropolitain French troops. Its right flank was protected by the Québec and part of the Montréal Militia. After the battle

1755: c.31 Officers
     515 NCOs and Men
May 1759: 489

12 Fusilier Companies
1 Grenadier Company
Uniform: grey white coat, lining and breeches, blue cuffs (three buttons) and collar, red waistcoat, brass buttons, gold hat lace.
Gold buttons for officers

Private, La Sarre Regiment, c. 1757-1760.
(Musée de l'Armée, Paris)

two officers and 40 men surrendered on 18 September, the survivors from the battalion retreating to Montréal.

In his recollections Captain de Merleval mentioned the many losses by the regiment on 13 September as comprising 'M. de Sénezergue, brigadier and battalion commander, and M. de Bourgnole, lieutenant (were killed). Messrs. de la Ferté, Savournin, Méritens, Despériers, Fleuriau, Laubanie and the Chevalier de Laubanie were wounded. There were about fifty men of the regiment, killed or wounded.'

Command of the regiment was now assumed by Messrs. de Lestang and de Fleurieau. The regiment saw more fighting in 1760. When it returned to France in October, 'there remained about 130 officers and men in the battalion ... Of 31 officers, ... 11 were killed and 20 wounded...'.

2ème Bataillon

LE RÉGIMENT DE ROYAL-ROUSSILLON

The regiment was raised in Roussillon and Catalonia from 26 May 1657. Its first colonel-in-chief was Cardinal Mazarin who was, in effect, the all-powerful prime minister of France during the youth of Louis XIV. It was first named 'Catalan-Mazarin' until the death of the cardinal in 1661, then 'Royal-Catalan' and finally, from 1667, 'Royal-Roussillon'. It was originally included in the 'Foreign' establishment of the French army because of its high proportion of Spanish Catalan recruits. Over time, its proportion of recruits from Roussillon and other parts of France increased so that, by the turn of the 18th century, it was

---

2nd BATTALION
ROYAL-ROUSSILLON REGIMENT
Lieutenant-Colonel Chevalier de Bernetz

---

an all-French regiment and no longer on the foreign establishment. The proportion of men recruited from Roussillon in this regiment remained high compared to other regiments with provincial names. Royal-Roussillon served in almost all of Louis XIV's campaigns. During the Seven Years' War, the 1st battalion was sent to Germany and was at Rossbach in 1757 and Bergen 1759.

Private, Royal-Roussillon Regiment, c. 1757-1760.
(Musée de l'Armée, Paris)

1755: c.31 Officers
        519 NCOs and Men
May 1759: 485

12 Fusilier Companies
1 Grenadier Company
Uniform: grey-white coat, lining and breeches, blue cuffs (six buttons), collar and waistcoat, brass buttons, gold hat lace.
Gold buttons for officers.

The regiment had a second battalion from 1701 until it was disbanded in 1715. Another second battalion was formed in Flanders in October 1746 and returned to France in 1748. It was in Brittany at the beginning of the Seven Years' War. Organised into the normal 13 companies, including one of grenadiers, it was ordered to New France with the new metropolitan army commander-in-chief, General Montcalm. With II/La Sarre Regiment, the battalion embarked in March 1756 at Brest and arrived safely at Québec in May. The unit was first posted in the Montréal area, with a detachment at Fort Carillon, and was not deployed for the attack on Oswego that year but remained to guard the southern approaches to Montréal. The unit winter-quartered in the Fort Chambly area by the Richelieu River, the traditional land invasion route into Canada. In 1757 the whole battalion travelled down Lake Champlain and Lake George with Montcalm's army to capture Fort William-Henry. A detachment was again left at Ticonderoga while the rest took up winter quarters between the villages Longueuil and Vercheres, south of Montréal. On 8 July 1758, some 460 men of Royal-Roussillon held the centre of Montcalm's line which defeated the repeated assaults of General Abercromby's Anglo-American army.

The battalion marched to defend Québec in May 1759 and took part in the battle of Montmorency and the battle of the Plains. Two officers and 39 men from the regiment were captured in the city on 18 September, the rest of the battalion retreating to Montréal.

2ème Bataillon
LE RÉGIMENT DE LANGUEDOC

The Languedoc Regiment was raised from 20 March 1672 and was named after the large southern French province. During the Seven Years' War, the 1st battalion was sent to Germany in 1758. It fought successfully at the battle of Hastembeck, but was in the defeated French army at Minden.

The 2nd battalion embarked at Brest in April 1755 along with the rest of the French metropolitan troops bound for New France. On the way, the *Lis* with four of its companies on board was captured by Boscawen's British fleet although war had not been declared. Most of the French fleet escaped and the other nine companies landed at Québec on 19 June. Languedoc was sent to Fort St Frédéric and, under General Dieskau, was repulsed at Lake George in September by Sir William Johnson and his New England militiamen. The French troops retired to Ticonderoga where Fort Carillon was built. Languedoc took its winter quarters that year in the Chambly area.

> 2nd BATTALION
> LANGUEDOC REGIMENT
> *Lieutenant-Colonel de Privat*

In May, the unit was back at Ticonderoga and with La Reine garrisoned there until October when most of the battalion moved into winter quarters in Montréal. A detachment of 50 men remained in garrison at Fort Carillon and part of this force was involved in the French defeat of Rogers' Rangers at La Barbue Rock on 21 January 1757. In March, nine grenadiers from the battalion took part in a raid on Fort William-Henry.

In July, Languedoc returned to Ticonderoga and from there moved south to take part in the siege and capture of Fort William-Henry in early August. Four companies, replacing those lost on the *Lis*, joined the battalion in September 1757. The regiment wintered in the St Augustin area and was back at Fort Carillon in June. On 8 July, the battalion helped defeat Abercromby's Anglo-American army, being posted on the left of the French line with La Sarre. 418 men were reported fit for duty in August. Languedoc remained at Fort Carillon until November when it went into winter quarters in the Trois-Rivières area.

In May 1759, the regiment went to Québec where it participated in its defence. It took part in the battle of

1755: 31 Officers
        525 NCOs and Men
May 1759: 473

12 Fusilier Companies
1 Grenadier Company
Uniform: grey-white coat, lining and breeches, blue cuffs (three buttons), collar and waistcoat, brass buttons, gold hat lace, horizontal pocket with three buttons on each side. Gold buttons for officers.

Private,
Languedoc Regiment,
c. 1757-1760.
(Musée de l'Armée, Paris)

Montmorency on 31 July and was at the battle of the Plains on 13 September, where it formed towards the centre of Montcalm's line. A detachment of three officers and 38 men were left in the city, surrendering on 18 September, the rest of the unit having retreated to Montréal.

The Languedoc fought on until the surrender of Montréal in September 1760. Out of the 556 officers and men who had come to Canada in 1755, only 51 remained.

FRENCH COLONIAL TROOPS AND MILITIAS

COLONIAL STAFF OF NEW FRANCE

New France had an elaborate administrative structure which was based on that of a French province in the Ancien Régime. The senior official was the governor-general who was also the senior military officer with command over regulars and militias as he held the rank of lieutenant-general. While no formal general staff existed, there was under the governor-general a commandant for the garrison of the independent companies of colonial troops, a chief King's engineer officer, and a commander of artillery, which formed a senior military staff. The governor-general was allowed a small personal guard whose captain acted as his Aide-de-Camp.

> *Pierre de Rigaud, Marquis de Vaudreuil*
> Governor General of New France
>
> *Captain Jean-Daniel Dumas*
> Commandant of Colonial Troops
>
> *Chevalier François Le Mercier*
> Commandant of Artillery
>
> *Nicolas Sarrebource de Pontleroy*
> Officer Commanding Ingénieurs du Roi
>
> *Intendant François Bigot*
> Commissaires

Pierre de Rigaud, Marquis de Vaudreuil (1698-1778) was the Governor-General of New France from 1755 to 1760. He was the son of a previous governor-general and the first Canadian-born officer to rise to the top position of the colonial administration.
(National Archives of Canada, C3708)

The major towns of Montréal and Trois-Rivières, as well as the colonies of Ile Royale (capital: Louisbourg) and Louisiana (capital: New Orleans), each had a local governor, a 'Lieutenant du Roi' (a lieutenant-governor) and a Town Major. The governor-general also held the post of governor of the city of Québec which otherwise also had a 'Lieutenant du Roi', a Town Major and a Captain of the Gates. In rural areas, the local militia captains were the military authority.

The administrative structure in addition also had a number of civilian officials who had a considerable impact on the military. The Intendant was the most senior official next to the governor-general and was very powerful as he presided over financial and judiciary matters. He had a subaltern staff of commissaries' and storekeepers which had a direct impact on the pay and supply to troops. He also oversaw the administration of justice in colonial courts which included criminal cases involving troops such as desertion. His importance was denoted by his small armed escort of uniformed 'Archers de la Marine' who were his own police constables.

Finally, there was the bishop as the senior religious official who oversaw the chaplains assigned to the colonial troops. In conjunction with the intendant, the bishop was responsible for the hospitals which were run by orders of nuns and which provided care to the military in return for a royal subsidy. Surgeons were appointed to a hospital on the same basis.

From 1755, with the arrival of metropolitan troops, some of this changed. Generally speaking, Vaudreuil had the last word on all matters relating to colonial troops and militias, diplomacy and strategic objectives. Montcalm had complete control over the metropolitan troops and tactics. Every effort was made to keep officers with their own types of troops. Otherwise, the

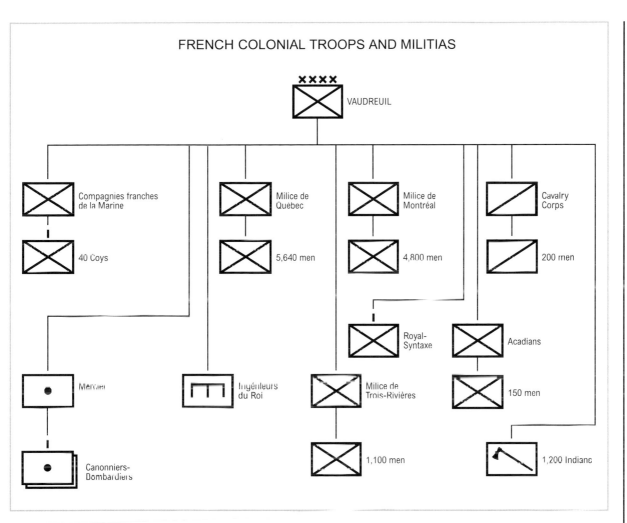

FRENCH COLONIAL TROOPS AND MILITIAS

XXXX
VAUDREUIL

Compagnies franches de la Marine

40 Coys

Milice de Québec

5,640 men

Milice de Montréal

4,800 men

Cavalry Corps

200 men

Mercier

Canonniers-Bombardiers

Ingénieurs du Roi

Royal-Syntaxe

Milice de Trois-Rivières

1,100 men

Acadians

150 men

1,200 Indians

senior officers would agree on a commandant of mixed troops. This does not seem to have caused major problems during the war. Thus, colonial Captain De Léry commanded metropolitan troops in 1756 and metropolitan Captain Pouchot was giving orders to colonial troops in 1759.

But otherwise, it was an awkward command structure and the mix between the colonial and metropolitan staffs could cause friction when it came to tactical and strategic choices.

In spite of many hardships suffered by the troops and the Canadian populace at large during the Seven Years' War, corruption and swindling of government accounts was rampant. This print illustrates the lavish parties of Intendant François Bigot, the French Crown's senior finance and administration official who should have prevailed against such abuses. He and his gang of knaves were roundly condemned but nothing much was done until New France had fallen.

Compagnies franches de la Marine

In New France, the 'Compagnies franches de la Marine' (Independent Companies of the Navy) were the regular garrison of colonial infantry They were named 'Compagnies franches' because they were not organised into regiments but as independent companies, and 'de la Marine' because they did not come under the Ministry of War but under the Ministry of the Navy, which was also responsible for the administration and defence of France's American colonies. They were often also called the 'Troupes de la Colonie' (Colony's Troops) in French chronicles. They had been posted permanently in Canada since 1683 and the officer corps had become an important part of the upper echelons of Canadian colonial society.

By the time of the 1759 siege of Québec, the majority of its officers were born in Canada and came from the families of the Canadian gentry. Many of the officers were masters at the peculiar tactics of wilderness warfare in North America, unfortunately much misunderstood and somewhat rejected by many metropolitan officers. The enlisted men were recruited in France and sent over for a period of military service after which they usually became settlers in Canada. Most of them were suited for ordinary military duties but a proportion was well versed in the intricacies of wilderness warfare. These regular colonial soldiers were routinely used as cadres for drafts of Canadian militiamen.

At the time of the siege of Québec, the colonial infantry troops of Canada had a theoretical establishment of 40 companies of 65 men each making 2,600 NCOs and privates led by 160 officers. However, they were much below strength for lack of recruits and were widely deployed usually in small detachments, standing guard in wilderness forts as far as present-day Saskatchewan.

In 1757, a temporary battalion of 500 men divided into eight companies was formed from some of these colonial troops to serve with Montcalm's metropolitan troops under those officers 'least fit' for bush warfare. This battalion was often termed 'Régiment de la Marine' by French metropolitan officers in their memoirs which confused some future historians. But it had, in fact, nothing to do with the senior metropolitan line infantry regiment named La Marine. It was the only unit of 'Compagnies franches' which carried a set of colours.

COMPAGNIES FRANCHES DE LA MARINE
(TROUPES DE LA COLONIE)

40 Companies each of 65 men

Uniform: grey-white coat, blue cuffs, lining, waistcoat and breeches, brass buttons, gold hat lace.
Officers had gold buttons.

Private, Compagnies franches de La Marine, the colonial regular infantry, c. 1758-1760. (Artist's impression by Eugène Lelièpvre, Parks Canada)

The exact number of colonial troops from the Compagnies franches de la Marine with Montcalm's forces during the siege is hard to pin down. There was a reserve of 600 of these troops on the left side of the French sector on the Beauport shore, not far from the Montmorency River. Unknown numbers were with the militias whose regular backbone and senior command they often provided. The grand total may have come to about 800 to 1,000 men.

Most of these colonial troops usually wore the grey-white faced blue uniform and were armed with muskets, bayonets and swords. However, those serving as skirmishers, officers included, usually wore Canadian costume armed with musket, tomahawk and knives.

Canonniers-Bombardiers

While there had been informal artillery units in New France since the 17th century, the first regular colonial artillery company, the 'Canonniers-Bombardiers', was formed at Louisbourg in 1743. More were formed in the West Indies in 1745 and 1747. Canada's turn came in 1750 when a company of Canonnier-Bombardiers was formed in Québec. It was joined by a second company in 1757. Since the end of the 17th century, some soldiers of the Compagnies franches had been trained as artillerymen by the 'King's gunner' later called the commissary of artillery. The new gunners were thus picked from the enlisted men in the colonial infantry who showed the most skill as gunners. The commissary of artillery, the Chevalier Le Mercier, was the commander of the Canonniers-Bombardiers in Canada. The new colonial artillery unit sent small detachments as far as the Ohio Valley but its home base was Québec.

CANONNIERS-BOMBARDIERS
Chevalier le Mercier

Small detachments of the metropolitan army artillery, the 'Corps Royal de l'Artillerie' or 'Royal-Artillerie', were sent to Canada during the war. In June 1757, six officers and 20 gunners landed at Québec; in May 1759 some 40 gunners, miners and sappers also arrived. These army gunners were joined to the colonial artillery companies but kept their army identity.

There were also other trained gunners besides these soldiers. The most able were probably the sailors, some trained in artillery, who were added to the garrison for service in the shore batteries from warships trapped in the harbour. For instance, the area to the west of the city's fortifications was manned by corvette Captain de Folign, with 140 sailor-gunners, serving 20 cannons and two large mortars. Québec militia artillerymen also formed a cadre of gunners for untrained militiamen assigned to serve the guns. Finally, there was also a company of 'Ouvriers' or artisans/sappers raised from Canadians since 1757 who served with the artillery. In all, there were about 2,000 men serving the French guns during the siege of Québec. Of these, there were probably about 300 regular gunners.

CANONNIERS-BOMBARDIERS

2 Companies each of:
4 Officers
50 gunners and bombardiers

Uniform: blue coat with red cuffs, turnbacks, waistcoat and breeches, white metal buttons.

CORPS ROYAL DE L'ARTILLERIE

6 Officers
60 gunners, sappers and miners

Uniform: blue coat with red collar, cuffs, turnbacks, waistcoat and breeches, brass buttons.
Gold buttons for officers.

Gunners of the colonial artillery, 'Canonniers-Bombardiers' (left) and the metropolitan army's Royal-Artillerie (right), 1759-1760.
(Artist's impression by Eugène Lelièpvre-Private Collection)

Ingénieurs du Roi

The military engineers serving in New France with Montcalm's army were drawn from two separate corps. Already in Canada before the arrival of the metropolitan troops in 1755 were the 'Ingénieurs du Roi' (the King's Engineers) which were attached to the Ministry of the Navy and were really a colonial corps of engineers. As well as their appointment as engineers, these officers also held an officer's commission in the Compagnies franches de la Marine which gave them military rank, status and pay.

A considerable part of their time was spent inspecting and designing fortifications. Another duty was to survey frontier routes and outposts from time to time. The work of colonial engineers, however, could and did also involve many plans for civilian structures, from windmills to churches, as they were usually the only available and qualified architects on the spot. The chief engineer in Canada during the Seven Years' War was Lieutenant-Colonel Nicolas Sarrebource de Pontleroy, an experienced officer who had spent many years in the metropolitan engineers before transferring to the colonial troops. His service in both corps must have greatly helped harmonious relations between officers and also with Montcalm who often despised colonial officers. The colonial engineers continued to exist in other French colonies well after the fall of Canada as they were amalgamated with the army engineer corps only in 1784.

INGÉNIEURS DU ROI
Nicolas Sarrebource de Pontleroy

Originally, all engineers paid by the French crown were 'Ingénieurs du Roi' in a separate department. Most were detached to serve with the metropolitan army, others with the Navy and the colonies while some specialised in road and public works. This lasted until 1743-1744 when most engineers in France were assigned to form a specific corps of army engineers. In 1755, the metropolitan army engineers were combined with the Corps Royal de l'Artillerie, a most unhappy and unworkable union which ended in 1758, the army engineers then regaining their own corps and independence.

From 1755, a few army engineers were sent to Canada and worked smoothly with the few colonial

At least four officers including Chief Engineer Pontleroy served with Montcalm's army at Québec. They were assisted by at least two 'map designers' (later became the corps of Cartographic Engineers).
There were no enlisted men.

Uniform: the Ingénieurs du Roi wore scarlet coat with blue cuffs, scarlet waistcoat and breeches, gold buttons set in pairs, tricorn laced with gold. The metropolitan army engineer corps had a blue coat with black velvet cuffs and scarlet lining, scarlet waistcoat and breeches, gold buttons (five to each cuff and pocket), gold laced hat.

engineers in the colony. In May 1759, army engineer officers de Caire, Robert and Fournier arrived in Québec from France and joined Pontleroy's staff. During the siege, Pontleroy and de Caire were especially active in all parts of the French lines and their services were often mentioned by Montcalm in his journal.

Officer of the colonial 'Ingénieurs du Roi' (King's Engineers) wearing the distinctive scarlet uniform.
(Artist's impression by Michel Pétard. Parcs Canada)

La Milice de Québec

The New France Militia was raised on a permanent basis from 1669 when King Louis XIV instructed the Governor-General to organise all able-bodied males fit to bear arms from age 16 to 60 into companies of militia. Each parish had a company, sometimes more if it was populous, and each company was commanded by a captain assisted by lieutenants, ensigns and sergeants. According to the royal instructions, they gathered for training once a month, which generally meant target shooting rather than drill, and all were to have their own arms and ammunition.

The duties were not only military but included taking census, reading decrees and aiding the civil power such as in the pursuit of criminals. Commissions were issued by the Governor-General and captains were prominent men in their communities. This simple organisation by parish, based on that of the Coast Guard Militia in France, permitted large-scale mobilisation at short notice. For expeditions, quotas of volunteers would be obtained from the companies. There were flaws of course, and many men were not well armed, but this system was generally quite effective.

QUÉBEC MILITIA
Colonel Pierre-Gilles Bazin

Each parish belonged to one of the three districts (called 'gouvernement') of Québec, Trois-Rivières and Montréal. Each district had a colonel assisted by majors concerned with administrative matters. In wartime, officers of the regular troops had overall command. Except for a few special companies in cities, the vast majority of Canadian militiamen had no uniforms and wore the comfortable and peculiarly Canadian costume. Officers were required to wear a gilt gorget and a sword.

The Québec District Militia was made up mostly of farmers with some fishermen living in villages on both shores of the St Lawrence, the rest being residents of the city. In 1759, they formed a total of 6,350 men able to bear arms. Some 5,640 men from the district were assembled at Québec City in June 1759. This number included the 840 men of the Québec City Militia. This urban militia included a special company of 'Milice de Réserve', organised since 1752, which was made up of well-to-do Québec city merchants led by the gentry.

> **QUÉBEC DISTRICT MILITIA**
> 4,800 all ranks.
>
> **QUÉBEC CITY MILITIA**
> 840 all ranks.
>
> 'Milice de Réserve' Uniform: scarlet, white cuffs and waistcoat.

It was uniformed which was most unusual in the Canadian Militia. There was also a militia artillery company in Québec City, specialised in garrison artillery service. They were also uniformed, probably in blue laced with red, like the regulars. A firemen's company was also organised during the siege to put out fires started by the British bombardment.

The number of militiamen mobilised to defend New France was the highest ever called to duty. Together with all the militiamen assembled at Québec were Montcalm's five metropolitan infantry battalions, which were short of men. Thus the order was given by

A gilt gorget worn by Pierre Trudelle, a Canadian Militia officer killed on 12 July 1759. (Musée des Ursulines, Québec. Photo R. Chartrand)

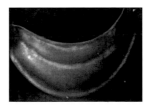

Governor-General Vaudreuil on 1 June 1759 to incorporate a number of militiamen into the five battalions for the duration of the campaign. Traditionally, Canadians were not keen on anything approaching regular service as soldiers, but they obviously relented, and about 600 – the exact figure is unknown – were attached to the five battalions. Each of the battalion's companies therefore had about ten militiamen drafted in, which included a sergeant and a corporal.

The largest concentration of Québec District Militia as a distinct unit was on the Beauport shore during the siege where some 3,000 militiamen were posted under the command of Pierre-Roch de Saint-Ours, an officer of the regular colonial troops.

La Milice de Trois-Rivières
La Milice de Montréal

MONTRÉAL MILITIA

The Montréal District Militia was reputed to be the best in New France owing to the fact that many of its men were voyageurs and fur traders. Most were farmers but some of them were given to occasional stints in the wood to seek game and a little trading with Indians. The result was a large proportion of men skilled in wood craft and thus better experienced in the wilderness and bush warfare.

This earned them the nickname of 'The Wolves' from disdaining citizens of Québec City, to which the Montréalers responded by calling them 'The Lambs'. In 1759, a total of 5,455 militiamen were mobilised in the Montréal District which included both the city and its surrounding area. About 4,800 men travelled from Montréal to help reinforce the garrison of Québec. This included an uncertain number of colonial troops. It must have been substantial because there were fears in Montréal that the many Anglo-American prisoners held there might overwhelm the small number of 'Compagnies franches' soldiers left to guard them. In all, possibly 600 to 800 might have been colonial troops.

> ### MONTRÉAL MILITIA
> *Colonel Joseph Prudhomme*
>
> ### TROIS-RIVIÈRES MILITIA
> *Colonel Louis de Bonne*

Thus, the number of Montréal militia present at the siege of Québec must have hovered around 4,000 to 4,200 men. Most were posted on the left flank of the French positions on the Beauport shore bordering the Montmorency River. Colonial troops captains Prudhomme and Herblain commanded the main body of Montréal militiamen. There was also an 800-man reserve under Captain Louis le Gardeur de Répentigny, a colonial troops officer who was a renowned expert in bush warfare. His reserve of Montréal militiamen likely gathered those most adept in woodcraft. Generally the Montréal militia were the best shots ·and it seems that they often loaded their muskets with a ball and six buckshots.

> ### TROIS-RIVIÈRES DISTRICT MILITIA
> 1,100 all ranks.
>
> ### Montréal District Militia
> 5,455 all ranks.
>
> The great majority of Canadian militiamen did not wear military uniforms but civilian utilitarian clothing used in Canada; the hooded coat called a "capot", usually grey or blue, with a waist sash; a wool cap which was usually red or blue; breeches or breechclouts; Indian style moccasins and leggings or leather boot-moccasins. Armament varied greatly but was basically a musket, a tomahawk and two or three knives.
> Militia officers, however, were required to wear a gilt gorget at all times and they were often armed with swords.

TROIS-RIVIÈRES MILITIA

The total number of militiamen mustered in the Trois-Rivières District and the small city of Trois-Rivières, half-way between Montréal and Québec, came to some 1,300 men in 1759. Most were farmers but a few would have been voyageurs in the fur trade. Others were craftsmen as the area was renowned for its fine canoes. A few of the men would have been workers from the St Maurice iron works. Most of the iron workers were likely to be kept at the forges as they produced ammunition, especially cannon balls, for the French forces.

Still, the Trois-Rivières District was practically devoid of its active male population during the siege as some 1,100 men were sent to Québec in June 1759. All of them were posted on the Beauport shore during the siege, under the command of Louis de Bonne, an officer in the regular colonial troops.

Following the fall of Québec, most of the Québec District militiamen laid down their arms, since their area was now under British control. However the Trois-Rivières and Montréal militias retreated in good order from Québec with Lévis' army. Some French metropolitan officers feared that the Canadians would become discouraged and give up, but they were ready to fight when called upon in the spring of 1760.

Royal-Syntaxe and the Acadians

Royal-Syntaxe was a militia company formed in June with the 35 students of the Québec Seminary who were able to bear arms. Hence its tongue-in-cheek name of Royal-Syntaxe given by Québec City jokers. The name immediately caught on and the company was recorded as 'Royal Syntaxe' in official French records! The seminary, founded in the 17th century, was the institution of higher learning in Canada and was not solely for aspiring priests as its name might suggest. It is today Laval University.

The services of the seminary students are not well documented but it is recorded that some of them took an undistinguished part in an abortive raid on the British position at Point Levy on 12 July 1759. A force of about 1,100 militiamen crossed over to the south shore under the command of Jean-Daniel Dumas and, as they neared the British position, some Royal-Syntaxe students mistook militiamen for British troops and opened fire. The militiamen, thinking it was a British ambush, ran off. Dumas cancelled everything and everyone returned to Québec where wags baptised the operation as the 'Coup des Écoliers' or The Schoolboys' Raid. Royal-Syntaxe thereafter disappears from the records.

ACADIAN MILITIA
Charles Deschamps de Boishébert

The 'Acadians' were especially experienced and hard-fighting men formed into a body of volunteers. Acadians were the original French settlers of Nova Scotia who had been deported by the British and New Englanders in 1755. These men had escaped the deportation by taking refuge in the forests of present-day New Brunswick. There, led by Charles Deschamps de Boishébert, a Canadian colonial officer from the Compagnies franches de la Marine, renowned for his guerrilla-style tactics who was sent from Canada to train them, they became skilled at partisan warfare which they waged relentlessly against the British posted on the border of Nova Scotia. Embittered Acadians such as Noël Brassard nicknamed 'Beausoleil', who had seen his wife and eight of his ten children die of exposure due to the 1755 deportation, learned especially well and became legendary in Acadian folklore because of the countless successful raids that

ROYAL-SYNTAXE MILITIA
1 Company of 35 men.

Uniform: wore the uniform of the students of the seminary, a blue capot (a coat with a hood) trimmed with white piping at the seams, white sash around the waist, plain tricorn hat.

ACADIAN MILITIA
100 men probably divided between 3 Companies.

Charles Deschamps de Boishébert was a handsome officer who was nicknamed 'le beau canadien' by the Acadians.

he, Boishébert and others staged with their men, all of whom sought vengeance from the Anglo-Americans.

Following the British incursions up the St John River with overwhelming forces during the fall of 1758 in an effort to contain the raids, a group of Acadians with allied Micmac Indians led by Boishébert went to Québec. About 150 Acadians were mustered at the siege of Québec with some Micmac Indians under Boishébert. On Wolfe's instruction, Dalling's light infantry tried to ambush them in mid-July but failed totally. Boishébert's Acadians and Micmacs formed one of the reserves at Montmorency, and skirmished on the outskirts of the Plains on 13 September. They later joined Lévis' army at Montréal.

CORPS OF CAVALRY

This corps was organised during June 1759 and has the distinction of being the very first unit of cavalry raised in Canada. It comprised 200 Canadian volunteers who were good horsemen led by five French metropolitan officers. The commandant of this corps was Montcalm's second ADC, Captain de La Roche-Beaucourt, formerly of the Montcalm Cavalry Regiment in France. The four subaltern officers were detached from the Béarn, Languedoc and Guyenne

---

CAVARY CORPS
Captain de La Roche-Beaucourt

---

regiments who had some previous experience in the cavalry. The corps was divided into two companies under the command of second captains, de Belcour and Louis-Jacques Ruelle de Santerre. It may be surprising to find good horsemen in colonial Canada but Canadians in the St Lawrence Valley loved horses and, by the first half of the 18th century, had considerable numbers of their favourite animal. By then, a peculiar breed of Canadian horse had evolved, small, sturdy, enduring and good-natured, a good draft and riding

Trooper

---

200 all ranks divided between 2 Companies.

Uniform – Other ranks: blue coats with red collar and cuffs, bearskin caps.

Uniform – Officers wore the uniform of their respective regiments.

---

horse. They also had all the expertise necessary to make the cavalry saddlery and horse furniture.

However, there was no need to have mounted units in the militia or the regular troops of New France until 1759 when Wolfe's army landed. Faced with a basically European-style siege campaign, the French officers saw the need to raise a regular mounted unit to serve with the army. The corps' duties called for a mixture of light cavalry, dragoon and even some heavy cavalry tactics. It was to patrol the shores of the St Lawrence, check enemy landings, fight on foot when required and provide dispatch riders. Montcalm recommended that the 200 volunteers be given a blue uniform, a bearskin cap 'to give them a martial look' and armed with sabres and good muskets. Accordingly, on 13 June, the corps was seen entering Québec City wearing 'a blue uniform with red collar and cuffs' and was reported well appointed. The officers were seen in white uniforms, no doubt those of their respective regiments.

The Canadian cavalry did not make grand charges during the campaign but it made its presence known by constant skirmishes with the British, who quickly came to respect this new addition to the French forces. It would appear that the troopers occasionally used their sabres when riding against the New England rangers as Knox mentioned a ranger being maimed by sword cuts.

Most of the corps served with Bougainville's force west of Québec. After the fall of the city, the corps retreated to Montréal with Lévis' forces and campaigned until disbanded following the surrender of Montréal in September 1760.

An officer and troopers of the Corps of Cavalry, 1759-1760. (Company of Military Historians)

The Indians

The defence of New France in the 17th and 18th centuries always depended largely on the Indian nations and the skills of Indian warriors. French settlers in Canada were more interested in exploration and trade than in colonising vast land areas and, as contact increased, partially adopted many of the Indian ways of transportation, clothing, food and tactics during the 17th century.

While the French had their Indian enemies, especially the Iroquois Six Nations in New York and the Fox in the west, they had far more allies from the Atlantic coast to the great plains west of the Great Lakes. French colonial diplomacy called for the usual respect by the Indians for the 'Great White Father' but equally respected the Indians as allies and brothers. The French government provided many valuable gifts. Canadian 'Compagnies franches de la Marine' officers were sent to spend time and live within the Indian nations, learning their languages, their ways and making steadfast friends.

The skulking 'Indian way of war' was well understood by the Canadian officers, such as Governor-General Vaudreuil and much less by General Montcalm and his metropolitan officers who always complained that they were undependable, might not obey orders, might commit cruel deeds and run off on the first occasion. The Indians, as Canadian officers well knew, were allies and not subalterns and always made it clear that they could not be ordered but had to agree to a plan. Being usually few in numbers, they abhorred casualties; in their type of warfare, it was paramount that losses be as few as possible, the exact opposite to European linear battle doctrine. Indians did not fight for pay but for glory and booty. Thus, they would move in – as they did at Montmorency – to take valuables and prisoners, which they would later sell, and to scalp. For the Indians, an enemies' scalp was a trophy The 'horrific practice' was loudly condemned by the Europeans while they offered money for scalps...

By 1759, many Indian nations could sense that the end was near for New France. Nevertheless, some 1,000 Indians were with the French forces at Québec in June 1759 and this number had risen to 1,775 at the height of the siege. A surprisingly large number, 983, came from the Great Lakes area – nearly 400 being Ottawas. Another 792 were from more eastern nations

Between 1,700 and 2,000 men.

Eastern woodland Indians, 1750s. The Indians had a mixture of their native dress and adornments, such as breeclouts, leggings and tattoos, combined with elements of European clothing, such as shirts and blanket coats in cold weather. The chief at the centre wears a plumed hat and scarlet coat laced with gold. (Canadian Dept. of Defence)

with nearly 400 Iroquois from the 'Five Nations of Canada' which were allied to the French.

While the Indians were involved in many skirmishes, they remained shy of general actions during the siege. During the battle of the Heights of Abraham they posed a constant threat to Wolfe's flanks and rear.

The loss of Québec convinced the Indian nations that the French would lose Canada. Therefore most sought arrangements with the British.

LA MARINE

I n the middle of the 18th century, France had, after Britain, the second most powerful navy in the world – 'La Marine'. It was but a shadow of the defiant and powerful navy of Louis XIV, however. Decades of neglect and 'laisser faire' by the successive governments of Louis XV had left it an inadequate fighting force. Its ships were technically advanced and its crews proficient and courageous but there were simply too few ships and sailors. As a result, sea routes to French colonies were constantly threatened and French squadrons were gradually swept off the seas during the Seven Years' War.

French ships still got through to Canada. In the spring of 1759, a small squadron under frigate Captain Jacques Kanon consisting of four frigates, the *Machault*, the *Maréchal de Senneterre*, the *Chézine*, all of 24 guns, and the *Manon* of 26 guns sailed from France escorting 14 armed transports. They were joined on the way by two more transports and by the frigates *Atalante*, *Marie*, *Pomone* and *La Pie* under the command of frigate Captain Jean Vauquelin. Three of the ships fell behind but 17 carrying some 13,000 barrels of flour, salt pork, wine, gunpowder, clothing and shoes all reached Québec safely during May. There were only 326 recruits to replace losses in the regular troops but the many sailors were a reinforcement and supplies were greatly welcomed.

FRENCH NAVAL FORCES
Captain Jean Vauquelin

They could not get out again as Admiral Durrell's stronger Royal Navy squadron was now in the St Lawrence River. A couple of frigates were stripped down and the rest of the ships were sent towards Trois-Rivières and further, some as far as Montréal. Their crews, about 2,000 sailors and officers, then returned to Québec to help defend the city.

About 1,400 were detached, mostly to serve with the artillery during the siege. The others – the 'worst' sailors according to La Pause – looked after the fire ships. There would also have been a relatively small number of marines, perhaps a hundred, from these ships. Two frigates, the *Pomone* and the *Atalante* under Captain Vauquelin, the senior officer, were kept west of the city of Québec but were no match for the stronger British

About **600 sailors** from warships trapped in Québec on general duties including fire ships.
About **1,400 sailors** from warships trapped in Québec serving as artillerymen.
About **100 Infantrie de la Marine.**

Uniform: officers had blue, faced with scarlet, gold buttons and lace.

ships when they ventured up to Batiscan during the siege. Kanon and Vauquelin, incidentally, were originally merchant captains who had been commissioned into the navy because there was a great shortage of experienced ship's officers. Kanon was certainly daring. In November, he managed to sneak past the British at Québec in his frigate the *Machault* with five other ships which all arrived safely in Brest on 23 December.

WOLFE'S COMMAND

The command of the army which was to attack Québec in 1759 went to the 32-year-old Brigadier-General James Wolfe. He was a young brigadier, with many other general officers senior to him in the army. However, appointments to senior command of important operations are always, in the end, decided by political authority in cabinet. The prime minister, William Pitt, was looking for a daring and professional officer to lead the expedition. He had already been forced to recall General Lord Loudoun in late 1757 because of bad luck and bad weather. The

---

Major-General James Wolfe
Officer Commanding

Brigadier-General Hon. Robert Monckton
2nd in Command and Officer Commanding 1st Brigade

Brigadier-General Charles Townshend
Officer Commanding 2nd Brigade

Brigadier-General James Murray
Officer Commanding 3rd Brigade

Colonel George Williamson
Officer Commanding Artillery

Major Isaac Barré
Adjutant-General

Colonel Guy Carleton
Quartermaster-General

Captain James Leslie
Assistant to the Quartermaster-General

Captain Caldwell
Assistant to the Quartermaster-General

Major Patrick Mackellar
Chief Engineer

Lieutenant-Colonel William Howe
Officer Commanding Light Infantry and Rangers

Captain Thomas Bell
ADC to General Wolfe

Captain Hervey Smith
ADC to General Wolfe

Major-General James Wolfe, in the all-red uniform he usually wore during the siege of Québec. He wears a black armband in memory of his father's recent death. (Print by J.S.C. Schaak after a sketch by Hervy Smith)

next year, he had relieved General Abercromby following the defeat of his army at Ticonderoga. In his place he had appointed, as commander-in-chief, Sir Jeffery Amherst, the methodical soldier who had taken Louisbourg. Pitt and his cabinet, knowing Amherst's cautious approach, put him in command of the army which would again attempt to wrest the Lake Champlain route from the French.

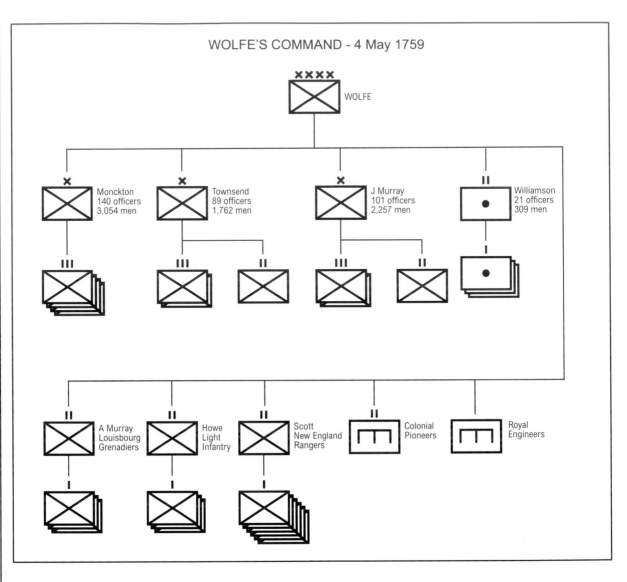

WOLFE'S COMMAND - 4 May 1759

xxxx WOLFE

x Monckton 140 officers 3,054 men

x Townsend 89 officers 1,762 men

x J Murray 101 officers 2,257 men

|| Williamson 21 officers 309 men

|| A Murray Louisbourg Grenadiers

|| Howe Light Infantry

|| Scott New England Rangers

Colonial Pioneers

Royal Engineers

To command the army that would take Québec was a challenge that Wolfe earnestly wanted. His gallantry at Louisbourg had been widely reported and lauded in the public press and in private military and political circles. This had given him his chance to shine in high places. Back in England, at the end of 1758, he lobbied for the command and won the support of Lord Ligonier, the Commander-in-Chief of the British army. Lord Ligonier next brought the idea of appointing Wolfe to Pitt. Wolfe could not have been aware of all the discussions going on about him behind closed doors. In early 1758 he was pessimistic, fearing that he might end up having to remain in England without a command. He was sickly and feared that this would go against him in the corridors of power. Pitt, however, agreed with Ligonier but the last thing to do was to win the agreement of King George II. The King liked the idea of appointing Wolfe and, on 29 December, Lord Barrington wrote to Wolfe advising him that His Majesty had approved his appointment to command the expedition. He was to have the rank of major-general for the duration of the campaign, after which time he would revert to brigadier.

More detailed instructions from the King came on 5 February 1759, which were the formal versions of what the government wished. Pitt was meanwhile ensuring that the Lords of the Admiralty made available a sizable portion of the Royal Navy and had arranged that the command of the fleet go to Vice-Admiral Saunders, a sailor of great experience. The cabinet feared the delays which had compromised previous expeditions, and Wolfe was instructed to be in Louisbourg by 20 April and that the expedition should sail from there on or about 7 May. He would report progress to Amherst and would especially send Pitt frequent, detailed reports of the operation.

Wolfe wished to appoint the three brigadiers who

Wolfe's Adjutant-General, Major Isaac Barré, in 1759. (Print from a portrait painted later in life.)

Colonel Guy Carleton, Quartermaster-General of Wolfe's army. He is shown in the uniform of his 72nd Foot. Carleton's future career in Canada was to be considerable as he was twice its Governor-General. (Private Collection)

would serve under him and chose Robert Monckton, James Murray and his friend Colonel Ralph Burton. Pitt approved the first two appointments but insisted that George Townshend should command a brigade instead of Burton. This was not due to a personal animosity towards Burton who was a good officer but the prime minister obviously wanted someone on the senior staff who did not owe his rank to Wolfe and could keep a discreet eye on him. Wolfe was disappointed but obviously understood the realities of senior command. And anyhow, he made sure Burton was part of the expedition.

Pitt was planning to assign a total of 12,000 regulars to Wolfe's campaign. Some of these troops were to be taken from various garrisons in America and would be replaced by New England provincial troops levied for the purpose. Only a few hundred colonial rangers and pioneers were allocated to be part of the expedition. It was obviously felt that only regulars would have a chance of success.

While preparations were going on in England, General Amherst was also making arrangements for the expedition from his HQ at New York. Lieutenants Montrésor and Peach of the Engineers were drafted in. Transport ships were chartered in American ports to provide an additional 6,000 tons capacity to the 20,000 tons of the fleet arriving from England. Smaller vessels were also requisitioned: some 70 whale boats and 40 schooners from Boston. At New York, work was going on to transform a merchantman into an hospital ship, manned with medical staff and supplies.

Provisions for such a large and possibly protracted campaign had to be secured. The navy and merchant vessels saw to their own supplies for the sailors. For the army, a contract was given on 26 March to the firm of Baker, Kirby and Baker for the supply of 12,000 troops in North America for six months. It specified that, for every seven days, each soldier was to be issued rations consisting of: seven pounds of bread or seven pounds of flour; seven pounds of beef or four pounds of pork; three pints of peas; one pound of cheese or six ounces of butter and half a pound of rice or a pound of flour. The firm was to be paid six pence per ration per day, with an advance payment of £36,000.

Quite apart from food, the expedition also needed staff and auxiliary services and these various postings were rapidly filled. Supervising administrative matters was Major Isaac Barré who was appointed as the expedition's adjutant-general. Barré was unknown to Wolfe but reputed to be an efficient officer and administrator. The two obviously got along well and Barré was one of the few officers who stayed on good terms with his commanding general during the campaign.

Colonel Guy Carleton, the quarter master-general of the expedition, had been a friend of Wolfe since at least 1753. Wolfe had tried, unsuccessfully, to have Carleton with him for the Louisbourg campaign but he now secured his services for the 1759 expedition. During the siege however, relations between the two strained their friendship. The other staff officers included Captain Hervey Smith, whose talent as an artist left us with fine pictures of the siege, and Captain Thomas Bell as aide-de-camp. Captains Caldwell and Leslie assisted Carleton. Captains Gwillam, Spital and Lieutenant Dobson were appointed majors of brigade.

For a siege, experienced engineers were crucial and Wolfe appointed Major Patrick Mackellar because of his knowledge of Québec. He was assisted by John Montrésor who also had much experience in North American campaigns, having arrived in 1755. It is interesting to note that he admired Wolfe but felt Brigadier Murray to be 'a madman'.

Colonel George Williamson was to command the large detachment of Royal Artillery. He had been in North America since 1757 and had directed the artillery at the siege of Louisbourg. The exact number of guns he had available to him during the expedition is not know but it was obviously an ample and varied train. Unlike the French, plenty of powder and ammunition was available to the British; 4,500 mortar shells and over 11,550 cannonballs were fired into Québec.

All these men, ships and supplies had to be brought together from various places in England and the American colonies to the rendezvous at Louisbourg. Wolfe had been instructed to sail by 7 May but he was already running late. He only reached Halifax with Saunder's fleet on 30 April, remained a few days to be appraised of the situation, and then sailed for Louisbourg, where he arrived on 15 May.

It is likely that only then did he realise that he had fewer than 9,000 regulars rather than the planned 12,000, but this does not seem to have greatly concerned him. He set about organising his army into three brigades, as originally intended, and on 4 May, issued orders for his initial brigade structure.

To avoid confusion and simplify identification, the fleet was divided into three divisions which equated to the brigades, with a flag system for the transport vessels to identify which troops they carried

Monckton's 1st brigade (White Division) had a plain white flag for Amherst's 15th Foot, white with one red ball for Kennedy's 43rd Foot, white with three red balls for Anstruther's 58th Foot, white with two blue balls for Fraser's 78th Foot (Highlanders).

Townshend's 2nd brigade (Red Division) had plain red for Bragg's 28th Foot, red with one white ball for Lascelle's 47th Foot, red with three balls for Monckton's 2nd Battalion of the 60th Foot.

Murray's 3rd brigade (Blue Division) had plain blue for Otways 35th Foot, blue with one ball for Webb's 48th Foot, blue with three balls for Lawrence's 3rd Battalion of the 60th Foot.

The Louisbourg Grenadiers had a flag half red and half white, the light infantry had half blue and half white, the rangers had red, white and blue horizontal stripes, the artillery had red top half over blue. There were other signal flags for various transports.

The composition of the three brigades lasted through the siege until 7 September, when Wolfe restructured them.

After the battle of 13th September, at 1800 hrs, the units were yet again re-brigaded as follows:

1st Brigade under Colonel Burton:
  Louisbourg Grenadiers
  Webb's 48th
  Monckton's 2/60th
  Lawrence's 3/60th
2nd Brigade under Colonel Fraser:
  Amherst's 15th
  Kennedy's 43rd
  Anstruther's 58th
  Fraser's 78th
3rd Brigade under Colonel Walsh:
  Bragg's 28th
  Otway's 35th
  Lascelles'47th.

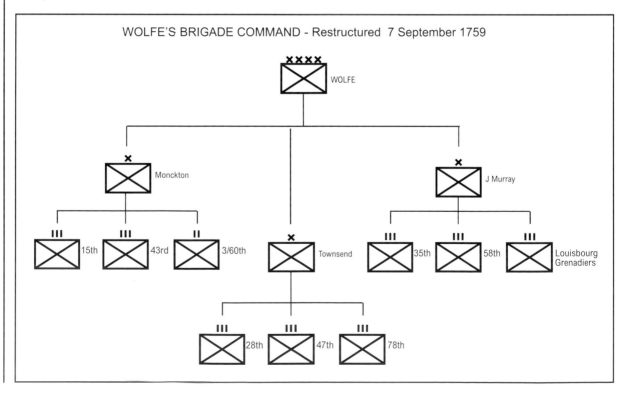

WOLFE'S BRIGADE COMMAND - Restructured 7 September 1759

WOLFE'S COMMAND

1st BRIGADE

An important factor in the expedition to Québec was the quality and experience of the senior officers who were with Wolfe. These were the three brigadiers Robert Monckton, James Murray and George Townshend.

The brigadier who was second-in-command after

15th Regiment of Foot
43rd Regiment of Foot
58th Regiment of Foot
78th (Highland) Regiment of Foot

Brigadier-General the Hon. Robert Monckton, c.1758. He wears the all scarlet undress uniform trimmed with gold buttons and gold laced waistcoat which was popular with officers.
(National Archives of Canada, C19118)

the border of New France west of Nova Scotia, the only British victories of the year. Later in 1755, he also had a part to play in a much less glorious episode: the deportation of the hapless Acadians. This terrible, repressive measure had been ordered by his superior, Governor Lawrence of Nova Scotia. The task consisted of arresting some 10,000 Acadians – the descendants of the French colonists who had settled in Acadia (now western Nova Scotia) – burning their farms and destroying their villages and deporting them as far away as possible on the American coast on board leaky ships. Monckton, a humane man who had been at odds before with Lawrence due to his heartless rigidity, had to obey.

This awful action, unworthy of the British, was later to inspire Longfellow's immortal and moving poem *'Evangeline'*. In all this, it would appear that Monckton and his soldiers were most reluctant and performed their duty with no enthusiasm. From December, Monckton was lieutenant-governor of Nova Scotia with occasional duties as governor. His main concern was the creation of a legislative assembly which was achieved in 1758. By then Monckton wanted less local politics and more military action. In the fall, he was put in command of a force of 2,300 men which went into the area of the St John River (in present day New Brunswick) to clear it of Acadians who had escaped deportation and become guerrillas. This was done by November although very few were taken; many went to Québec. Monckton too was to go to Québec.

In January 1759, Amherst called him to New York and envisaged giving him command of the troops in the south. But Wolfe was in New York too and recognised,

Wolfe was Robert Monckton, born in Yorkshire on 24 June 1726, the second son of Lady Elizabeth Manners and John Monckton who later became the 1st Viscount Galway. At age 15, in 1741, young Robert Monckton entered the 3rd Foot Guards as a subaltern and went to Flanders with his regiment. He was present at the battles of Dettingen in 1743, and Fontenoy in 1745 remaining with the British contingent in Flanders until 1748. In June 1744 he became a captain in the 34th Foot and major in 1747.

He remained in the army after the war and became lieutenant-colonel of the 47th Foot in 1752. That year, Monckton was sent to Nova Scotia. In June 1755, he led the British operations which led to the capture of the French forts Gaspareau and Beauséjour which guarded

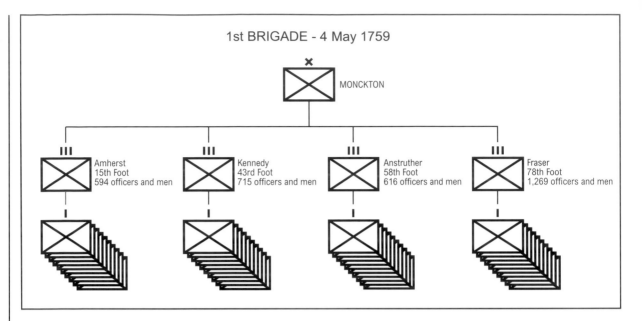

MONCKTON

Amherst
15th Foot
594 officers and men

Kennedy
43rd Foot
715 officers and men

Anstruther
58th Foot
616 officers and men

Fraser
78th Foot
1,269 officers and men

in Monckton, a very able officer. He offered him the post of brigadier on the Québec expedition. It was eagerly accepted.

Monckton, who was destined to play an important part in the Québec campaign, was also designated as second-in-command after Wolfe and thus the senior of the three brigadiers. He therefore headed north to join the army assembling at Louisbourg.

On 4 May, his brigade, which was numbered the 1st Brigade, was ordered formed. It consisted of Amherst's 15th, Kennedy's 43rd, Anstruther's 58th and Fraser's 78th Highlanders. It was important to get the units to work smoothly with each other and to practice landings. Monckton's men went to it and Captain Knox of the 43rd later related in his journal that 'The first brigade of the army, with the Louisbourg grenadiers, landed to-day (30 May near Louisbourg) for exercises; they performed several manoeuvres in presence of general officers, such as charging in line of battle, forming the line into columns and reducing them; dispersing, rallying and again forming in columns. and in line of battle alternately, with several other evolutions; which were all so well executed, as to afford the highest satisfaction to the generals... The troops have been daily engaged in these exercises, whenever the weather permitted.'

Upon arrival at Québec, Wolfe wished to secure the heights of Point Levy directly opposite the city on the south shore of the St Lawrence. Accordingly, Monckton's 1st Brigade with its four regiments was landed at Beaumont on the morning of 30 June. Small parties of Canadian skirmishers were easily swept away and Point Levy was soon dominated by the soldiers of the 1st Brigade. Good use was made of the pickaxes,

spades, shovels and billhooks issued to each regiment as many men were now put to work constructing the batteries which would bombard Québec. Once the batteries were in operation, it was Monckton who supervised them for Wolfe during July, transmitting Wolfe's orders to the Royal Artillery.

By the middle of July, there was much movement as a landing place was being sought. On 16 July, regiments were instructed to be ready to board boats except Amherst's 15th Foot which would guard Point Levy. The light infantrymen of Kennedy's 43rd were sent to Ile d'Orléans with those of Webb's 48th; those of Amherst's 15th were sent with 200 rangers to the Chaudière River.

At the end of July, the grenadier companies were detached to form a corps of shock troops for the assault on the Beauport shore at Montmorency.

During August, Wolfe took many detachments from Monckton's brigade, as well as putting part of the countryside to the torch, which Monckton much resented. Wolfe prized Monckton's friendship, and made some amends to Monckton on 15 August so that, as a whole, his relations with him were better than with the other two brigadiers.

On 7 September, the 1st Brigade composition changed to: Amherst's 15th, Kennedy's 43rd and Lawrence's 3rd Battalion 60th. There were further brigade changes after the 13 September battle of the Plains where Brigadier Monckton was badly wounded. Colonel Ralph Burton then assumed command. The 1st Brigade was eventually dissolved in October when some of the troops left Québec.

15th REGIMENT OF FOOT

The 15th Foot was one of the older regiments of the British line infantry as it was raised during 1685 in the Nottingham area. It had a distinguished record with Marlborough's army which included the battles of Blenheim, Ramillies, Oudenarde and Malplaquet. Its first service in America was in the unfortunate expedition against the Spanish at Cartagena de Indias (now in Columbia) in 1740. It later served in Flanders and against the Jacobite Highlanders in Scotland.

In September 1746, the 15th was selected to be part of a naval expedition sent to raid the French port of L'Orient, in Brittany, then an important harbour as it was the main base of the French East India Company's ships for its African and Asiatic trade. James Murray, who was later to win fame in Canada, was then the captain of the 15th's grenadier company. The expedition's leaders committed a series of blunders and accordingly the landings met with resistance from the French Coast Guard militiamen of Brittany. By early October, the raiders had finally reached the walls of L'Orient but by then they faced over 8,000 militiamen backed by over a thousand regulars and sailors. The British force retreated, its rearguard including Murray and his grenadiers to fend off the approaching French.

15th REGIMENT OF FOOT
Colonel Jeffery Amherst

At the beginning of the Seven Years' War, the 15th was again assigned to a naval raid against Rochefort, the large French naval base on the Atlantic, which also ended in what has been termed a 'discreditable fiasco.' But better days were ahead for the regiment.

From 22 May 1756 to 21 September 1768, the colonel was Jeffery Amherst. In 1758, the regiment was ordered to North America arriving in Halifax in May to participate in the expedition against Fortress Louisbourg. Here it was led by its colonel, General Amherst. In early June, some 763 officers and men of the 15th arrived with the rest of the army in Admiral Boscawen's fleet off Louisbourg. The grenadiers of the 15th were part of the landing force which 'pursued them [the French] almost to the gates' according to Captain Knox. The French garrison was completely surrounded but resisted valiantly for many weeks under heavy

---

34 Officers
560 NCOs and Men

8 Fusilier Companies
1 Grenadier Company
1 Light Infantry Company

Uniform: red with yellow facings, white lace with two black and yellow lines, pewter buttons.
Silver buttons and lace for officers.

---

bombardment. The grenadiers of the 15th, with those of other regiments, were in the forward lines of trenches which got closer to the walls of Louisbourg with every passing day. With no hope of relief, Louisbourg surrendered on 26 July.

Amherst's 15th was sent to destroy the French settlements in the Gaspé area in the autumn and was then ordered to Halifax.

In the spring of 1759, the 15th Foot was again sent to Louisbourg to be part of General Wolfe's army forming there for the expedition to Québec. Upon arrival at Québec they landed and set up camp on the south shore. Even that could be a risky business at times as the following incident illustrates. French floating batteries came within range of the 15th and 78th on 1 July and 'they cannonaded us for about half an hour' says Malcom Fraser who added that 'one sergeant of the 15th Regiment and eight of the Colonel's Company were knocked down with one ball, behind the Colours, and all wounded, two I believe, mortally.'

Some 594 officers and men of the 15th embarked Admiral Saunders' fleet in June and 406 were present at the battle of the Plains on 13 September.

Following the capture of Québec, Murray retained the 15th with him in the fortress city. The regiment was at the surrender of Montréal in September 1760. It then went to Crown Point and was sent to participate in the capture of Martinique and Havana in 1762. The 15th returned to garrison Québec in 1763 and Montréal and its surrounding area from 1765 until it at last sailed for home in May 1768.

43rd REGIMENT OF FOOT

The regiment was raised in 1741, served in Minorca and Flanders and was numbered 43rd from 1747. From 7 February 1746 to 24 March 1761, the colonel was Lieutenant-General James Kennedy. In 1756 the 43rd was in Ireland. During May 1757, it sailed over 700 strong with six other regiments for Halifax, Nova Scotia, where it arrived at the end of June.

In August, the regiment was ordered to garrison the western part of Nova Scotia, in what was one of the more thankless postings in North America. This area, originally named Acadia, had been colonised by French settlers in the 17th century and ceded to Britain in 1713. The deportation of the Acadians, far from settling the problem of Canadian and Indian raids from present-day New-Brunswick, made matters far worse. Embittered Acadians who had escaped deportation joined the Canadians and Indians and waged such an all-out

---

29 Officers
686 NCOs and Men

8 Fusilier Companies
1 Grenadier Company
1 Light Infantry Company

Uniform: red with white facings, white lace with two red lines and blue stars between, pewter buttons. Silver buttons and lace for officers.

> ### 43rd REGIMENT OF FOOT
> *Lieutenant-General James Kennedy*

Grenadier, Kennedy's 43rd Foot. British army grenadiers were distinguished by the highly-decorated mitre caps, wings at the shoulders and brass match cases on their pouch shoulder belt. (Watercolour by Cecil C.P. Lawson after David Morier. Anne S.K. Brown Military Collection, Brown University. Photo R. Chartrand)

partisan war that it took at least three British and New England regiments in western Nova Scotia to protect the rest of the province and Halifax from incursions. As winter approached, the 43rd Foot had six companies at Annapolis with the rest parcelled into a string of forts along the Bay of Fundy up to the isthmus of Chignectou, which connected the province to the mainland.

For the next 22 months, the regiment was on what was a difficult and depressing duty, being constantly on the look-out for lone snipers or an ambush. Even wood-cutting details had to be escorted. Isolated soldiers who ventured out too far and were not accounted for by the time the roll was called were usually found by search parties in a nearby wood, scalped.

A low ebb was reached when the regiment was not selected to take part in the 1758 Louisbourg expedition. Captain Knox reported the news being received with 'not only a great disappointment, but an unspeakable mortification to the 43rd regiment, thus doomed to an unsoldierly and inactive banishment'. Six of its companies replaced the 28th Foot at Fort Cumberland (the former French Fort Beauséjour). With other regular troops, the unit took part during the autumn in a partly successful expedition up the St John River to destroy partisan bases.

At last, in April 1759, the regiment was ordered to sail for Louisbourg for the Québec expedition, arriving in May. All ranks were in 'such good spirits (at) going on immediate service' noted Knox.

Some 327 members of the regiment were present at the battle of the Plains on 13 September where they were in the centre of Wolfe's battleline.

58th REGIMENT OF FOOT

The 58th Foot was raised in England from December 1755 by Lieutenant-General Robert Anstruther who was its colonel until 14 December 1767. The regiment assembled at Gloucester early in 1756 and remained in England until the following year when it was sent to Ireland. Raised as the 60th, the regiment was renumbered the 58th on 8 February 1757. During the same month orders were given for the regiment to proceed to board ships headed for North America. The 58th went to Cork and sailed from Ireland in late March 1758.

Once in North America, the 58th was selected as part of the force to take part in the siege of the Fortress of Louisbourg. It was assigned to Lieutenant-Colonel Charles Lawrence's right wing. For the regiment, this assignment was especially important. It was a newly-raised unit and this campaign would be the

---

58th REGIMENT OF FOOT
Lieutenant-General Robert Anstruther

58th's baptism of fire — its first time in battle. Some 785 all ranks under Lieutenant-Colonel Howe embarked in Admiral Boscawen's fleet which sailed out of Halifax on 28 June, part of a force of some 12,000 troops on the 157 ships of the expedition's fleet. On 8 June, the nine

Private, Anstruther's 58th Foot, 1759, shown in campaign order with brown marching gaiters and full equipment.
(Artist's impression by G. Embleton. National Historic Sites, Parks Canada)

---

27 Officers
589 NCOs and Men

8 Fusilier Companies
1 Grenadier Company
1 Light Infantry Company

Uniform: red with black facings, buff lining, brass buttons and yellow lace.
Gold buttons and lace for officers.

---

battalion companies were part of a feint attack against Pointe Blanche while the grenadier company was part of the forces that landed with Wolfe and secured Kensington Cove. Thereafter, Anstruther's 58th all landed with the rest of the army and helped secure the heights upon which the British batteries were installed. The town was soon surrounded by the British forces and surrendered on 26 July.

The 58th gave good service during the siege of Louisbourg but did not have the chance to distinguish itself. This opportunity would come the next year. Following the surrender of Louisbourg, Anstruther's 58th was sent to Halifax where it remained in garrison until the spring of 1759. In May, the regiment went back to Louisbourg to join the army assembling there under General Wolfe.

Some 335 of the 58th were present at the battle of the Plains on 13 September. The regiment was one of several units which remained in garrison at Québec during the winter of 1759. It was part of General Murray's army during the final advance, with two other British armies, on Lévis' troops. Following the surrender of Montréal, it was sent west to garrison forts on the Great Lakes.

In 1762, it was called back to be part of the force under Lieutenant-General Burton which was dispatched from New York to take part in the expedition against the Spanish at Havana, Cuba.

Following the fall of the Cuban capital, the 58th remained there until 1763 when the city reverted to Spain by the Treaty of Paris, and the regiment returned to Ireland.

78th (HIGHLAND) REGIMENT OF FOOT

This regiment of Highlanders was raised in Scotland from January 1757. It was under the command of Lieutenant-Colonel the Honourable Simon Fraser, Master of Lovat who was chief of Clan Fraser. Nearly all its 41 officers were commissioned in January and included some 15 Frasers followed by 13 MacDonalds or MacDonells, six Camerons and six Campbells, many of whom were related to each other. It was a very strong regiment with 40 sergeants, 20 drummers and pipers, 987 other ranks with another 130 as supernumerary by April 1757. It had ten companies and obviously had no enlistment problems. In July 1757, three additional companies were authorised to be raised. A year later, the strength had risen to 82 officers and 1,460 enlisted men for a total of 1,542. It seems most of the enlisted men spoke in and understood only Gaelic.

The regiment was first numbered the 63rd and was also sometimes termed the Second Highland Battalion (the first being Montgomerie's 62nd Highlanders). On 21 April, the regiment was renumbered 78th.

In October, ten companies of the regiment sailed from Ireland for North America and spent the winter quartered in Connecticut. The three additional companies joined the regiment in March 1758. All went to Boston and in April sailed for Halifax where an army under General Amherst was assembling to attack Louisbourg. It was put in General James Wolfe's left wing for the attack.

78th (HIGHLAND) REGIMENT OF FOOT
Colonel Simon Fraser

On 8 June the 78th Highlanders were among the troops landing at Coromandière cove near the town. The fire from French outposts was brisk but the landing was successful. Thereafter, there were a few skirmishes involving the 78th until Louisbourg surrendered on 26 July. Fraser's 78th lost four officers killed, three wounded and 67 rank and file killed or wounded during the siege. After wintering in New England, the 78th returned to Louisbourg for the expedition to Québec. 672 were present at the battle of the Plains on 13 September. The 78th was one of the regiments selected to remain in garrison at Québec.

---

50 Officers
1,219 NCOs and Men

8 Fusilier Companies
1 Grenadier Company
1 Light Infantry Company

Uniform: red faced with white, belted plaid and kilts. The tartan is unknown. Grenadiers of Highland regiments had bearskin caps.
Gold buttons and lace for officers.

Two officers of the 78th Foot (Fraser's Highlanders), 1759-1760. This detail from a print is possibly the only period representation of the unit. Fraser's peculiar dress naturally caused amazement and comments among Canadians. The regiment remained in Canada until disbanded in 1763. Some 158 men with a few officers, out of about 500, stayed on as settlers.
(National Archives of Canada, C361)

WOLFE'S COMMAND

2nd BRIGADE

George Townshend was born into the nobility in 1724, the eldest son of Audrey Harrison and George, 3rd Viscount Townshend, wealthy owner of extensive estates in Norfolk. After studies at Cambridge, he joined the army as a volunteer in 1742 and served as a staff officer with Lord Dunmore in

28th Regiment of Foot
47th Regiment of Foot
2nd Battalion, 60th Regiment of Foot
(The Royal American Regiment of Foot)

Brigadier-General George Townshend.
(Print after Muller. National Archives of Canada, C8674)

Germany. In 1745 he was commissioned captain in the 20th Foot and was present at the battle of Culloden in April 1746. He then became ADC to the Duke of Cumberland in 1747 and was at the battle of Laffeldt. The next year, he became captain in the Foot Guards, a rank which automatically made him a lieutenant-colonel in the rest of the army.

After the war ended in 1748, he became embroiled with the Duke of Cumberland and, elected as Member of Parliament for Norfolk, made bitter attacks on the King's son in the House as well as devastating caricatures, Townshend being also a gifted artist. He resigned from the army in 1750. Most of his activity in the next years was getting a militia bill passed in Parliament which was done largely through his efforts in 1757. That year, the Duke of Cumberland was replaced as commander-in-chief of the army by Lord Ligonier and Townshend returned to the forces in May 1758 as a colonel unattached to any unit. This well-connected and influential nobleman was obviously an able soldier. Lord Ligonier selected him to be appointed by Pitt as one

of the brigadiers of the Québec expedition. As Wolfe had specifically asked that he would be free to choose all his brigadiers, and indeed had his friend Ralph Burton in mind for the job rather than Townshend, it must have come as a disappointment and caused some resentment. On the other hand, it stands to reason that Ligonier and Pitt wanted one of the senior officers to be critically and politically accountable to themselves rather than to Wolfe.

Of the three brigadiers, Townshend was junior to Monckton but superior to Murray and so was technically the third in command of the expedition. He crossed the Atlantic with Wolfe in early 1759 on board Vice-Admiral Saunders' HMS *Neptune*. Naturally, he was the least likely to show considerable deference and respect to Wolfe whom he seemed to have considered as something of an upstart. Townshend made biting caricatures of his commander but also one of the best and frankest portraits of Wolfe in watercolours.

Once in Nova Scotia, Townshend was assigned command of a brigade on 4 May. His brigade, numbered the 2nd, consisted of Bragg's 28th, Lascelle's 47th and Monckton's 2nd Battalion of the 60th. Most of the month of May was spent training at Louisbourg for the landings by the brigades of Wolfe's army. By the end of the month, they were considered proficient enough at it and, at the beginning of June, the army boarded the fleet and sailed from Louisbourg towards Québec. Townshend's 2nd Brigade was assigned as the Red Division, the transports on which the regiments had embarked having red flags with various regimental distinctions. At the end of the month, the fleet had reached Québec.

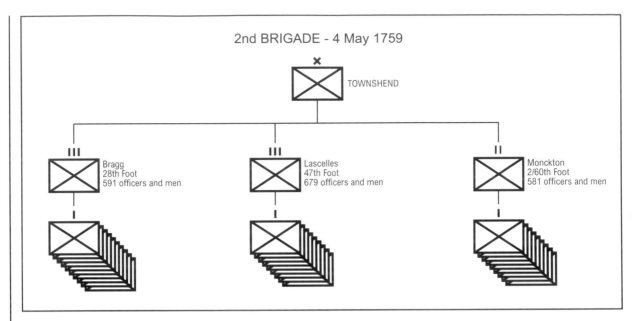

2nd BRIGADE - 4 May 1759

TOWNSHEND

Bragg
28th Foot
591 officers and men

Lascelles
47th Foot
679 officers and men

Monckton
2/60th Foot
581 officers and men

A sketch of General Wolfe by George Townshend, presented by the artist to Isaac Barré.

Once the heights of Point Levy were secured, Wolfe sought a landing place on the north shore. The Beauport shore, where he had initially hoped to land troops, proved to be strongly fortified and manned by thousands of French soldiers, Canadian militiamen and Indians. Although suffering from a bout of sickness, Wolfe studied his maps again and resolved to land east of the Montmorency River on the north shore. The idea was to draw the attention of the French on that front so that other operations elsewhere would be made easier.

On 4 July, Townshend's 2nd Brigade was ordered to be ready to land 'below the Fall of Montmorency to draw the Ennemys attention that way' which produced the first important disagreement between Wolfe and Townshend. Apparently, Brigadier Townshend had not been consulted on this move and obviously did not agree with Wolfe's manners nor his tactical move. Wolfe mentions a 'difference of opinion' with an unnamed 'inferior officer' who threatened him with a 'Parliamentary Inquiry Into his Conduct' which only Townshend could have done. The 'difference of opinion' was in all probability about the division of the British forces this move would cause.

But Wolfe would have none of it and ordered the landing of the 2nd Brigade which occurred on 9 July. There was no opposition at all from the French and the men immediately began entrenching and building some sizable field fortifications on the east side of the Montmorency. As it turned out, Townshend's reluctance to establish a camp there was correct. The French senior officers were satisfied as they quickly saw that the division of forces only lessened the chances of a strong attack. Montcalm thereafter made sure to keep pressure on the Montmorency camp by constant harassment by Canadians and Indians but never wished to attack it.

During July and August, detachments were routinely drawn from the 2nd Brigade for various operations including the abortive attack below the Montmorency Falls. Other detachments took part in the burn and pillage excursions of August which were deeply disturbing to Townshend, who by now, was on very cold terms with his commanding general.

At last, in early September, Wolfe finally pulled out of Montmorency and sent the 2nd Brigade to Ile d'Orléans. On 7 September, its composition was changed. Following the death of Wolfe and with Monckton badly wounded, Townshend assumed command of the army and the 2nd Brigade went to Colonel Fraser and now included the 15th, 43rd, 58th and 78th regiments. It was eventually dissolved with the departure of some of the regiments in October.

28th REGIMENT OF FOOT

The 28th was first raised in England during 1694 as Gibson's (or Gibbon's) Regiment. Of all the regiments with Wolfe's army, it was the one that had the most ancient links with North America. In 1697, Gibson's was the first British line regiment to be posted in what is now Canada, at St John's, Newfoundland, to protect it against French raids. The regiment left in 1698 but many men remained as independent garrison companies which became ultimately the 40th Foot from 1717. From 10 October 1734 to 24 October 1759, the colonel was Lieutenant-General Philip Bragg who was succeeded by George Townshend.

The 28th returned to North America, sailing from Cork in Ireland in early May 1757 and arrived at Halifax, Nova Scotia, in late June. It remained in Halifax until the fall when sent to garrison Annapolis Royal and Fort Cumberland on the western border of Nova Scotia. In early May 1758, the 28th Foot was sent to Halifax to be part of the army assembling under General Amherst for the expedition against Louisbourg.

28th REGIMENT OF FOOT
Lieutenant-General Philip Bragg

On 30 May, 650 men of Bragg's 28th sailed on board the fleet carrying the 12,000-strong British force deployed against Louisbourg. It was part of Brigadier Lawrence's right wing and its grenadiers, followed by the rest of the regiment, landed on 8 June. It then took part in the siege and was often noted in the trenches which were getting closer to the walls of the fortress under the direction of Brigadier-General Wolfe. On 23 July, a new battery position very close to the town's defences was built during the night and manned by various detachments including troops from Bragg's 28th. It came into action against the King's Bastion. The French responded with heavy fire but this slackened when another new battery position, also just built nearby, was brought into play. By the morning of 26 July, the breach in the wall was almost practicable and was being enlarged to allow the general assault which led to the surrender of the town later that day.

The 28th remained in garrison at Louisbourg with the 22nd, 40th and 45th regiments until the summer of 1759. The other three regiments remained at Louisbourg but the 28th Foot was selected for General Wolfe's assault on Québec.

591 all ranks of the regiment embarked in June and 421 were present at the battle of the Plains on 13 September. Following the surrender of Québec, Bragg's 28th remained in Canada. In the spring of 1760, Murray was beaten at Sainte-Foy but his force was not destroyed. Soon the British had received considerable reinforcements by land and sea. The regiment was part of Murray's army which combined with two other armies outside Montréal, forcing the city's surrender in September 1760.

The 28th remained in Montréal until 1761 when it sailed for Barbados to join a large British force. In January 1762, it took part in the capture of Martinique and, in June, was part of the force which took Havana. The regiment was part of the British force that was left to occupy the Cuban capital and the 28th remained in Havana until 1763 when the island was handed back to Spain in exchange for Florida.

Its service in America was still not over yet and the 28th was sent back to be part of the garrison of Canada. It was in Montréal until 1767 when it was finally ordered to return to England. It is interesting to note that, when inspected the following year, the regiment was found to still have an unofficial 'Light Infantry Company' which was seen 'clothed in short coats and caps'.

---

26 Officers
565 NCOs and Men

8 Fusilier Companies
1 Grenadier Company
1 Light Infantry Company

Uniform: red with bright yellow facings, white lace with two yellow lines and two black zigzag lines and black dots, pewter buttons.
Gold buttons and lace for officers.

47th REGIMENT OF FOOT

The regiment was originally raised in 1740 as Mordaunt's 58th Regiment, but was renumbered 47th in 1748. From 13 March 1743 to 2 April 1772, the colonel was General Peregrine Lascelles. It served against the Jacobites in 1745-1746. Four years later, the 47th sailed from Ireland to Nova Scotia and, by August, was posted at Fort Lawrence on the western border of Nova Scotia, near the French forts of Beauséjour and Gaspareau. In 1755, it participated in the capture of these French forts and also in the unsavoury duty of deporting the Acadians. The 47th was in Nova Scotia until 1758 when it participated in the capture of Louisbourg.

Before the battle of Montmorency, Sergeant Ned Botwood of the 47th's grenadier company was in high spirits. He sensed something was about to happen. An amateur poet, he penned the following lines:

47th REGIMENT OF FOOT
General Peregrine Lascelles

Private, Lascelles' 47th Foot, 1759. (Artist's impression by G. Embleton. (Canadian Dept. of Defence)

---

36 Officers
643 NCOs and Men

8 Fusilier Companies
1 Grenadier Company
1 Light Infantry Company

Uniform: during the 1759 campaign, the 47th did not have its regulation dress of red, faced with white, which had been captured by a French privateer. It was issued with uniforms meant for Shirley's 50th and Pepperel's 51st disbanded regiments.
These uniforms were red, faced with red, and trimmed with plain white lace, pewter buttons.
Presumably, the officers wore their regimentals of scarlet faced with white, probably silver buttons and lace.

'When the Forty-seventh Regiment is dashing ashore,
While bullets are whistling and cannons do roar,
Says Montcalm: "Those are Shirley's, I know the lapels."
"You lie," says Ned Botwood, "we belong to Lascelles!
Tho' our cloathing is changed, yet we scorn a powder-puff;
So at you, ye bitches, here's give you Hot Stuff'.

Sergeant Botwood's prose, since made famous, had a few lines which may seem obscure today. He mentioned that Montcalm would recognise 'Shirley's'. This referred to the fall of Fort Oswego to Montcalm in 1756. Shirley's 50th Foot was part of the captured garrison. He therefore knew the uniform's lapels which were in the regimental facing colour, red for Shirley's. The 47th had white lapels but their uniforms had been captured in late 1758. Shirley's 50th had been disbanded but their new uniforms had been shipped to New York. They were issued to the 47th as its 1759 clothing. Thus the regimental pride in Botwood's poem – they were clothed as the lacklustre 50th but were Lascelles' brave 47th "dashing ashore" to give "Hot Stuff".

360 men of the 47th Foot were present at the battle of the Plains on 13 September, where they occupied the centre of Wolfe's battleline.

2nd Battalion – 60th FOOT
(THE ROYAL AMERICAN REGIMENT OF FOOT)

The 60th Regiment of Foot 'or Royal American Regiment of Foot' was authorised to be raised in the American colonies from 24 December 1755 and was numbered the 62nd until renumbered the 60th in August 1756. The Colonel-in-Chief was the Earl of Loudoun until 27 December 1757, then General James Abercromby who was replaced by General Amherst on 30 September 1758. It was an unusual unit compared to other regiments of British line infantry. Most British regiments had one battalion but the 60th was allowed to recruit four battalions but, then again, this regiment was not quite British. Even its uniform was somewhat different from the rest of the infantry, the men's coats not being trimmed with any regimental lace.

It had been raised as a result of a suggestion to the Duke of Cumberland, commander in chief of the British army, from Colonel James (or Jacques) Prévost, a Swiss soldier of fortune. The initial scheme called for the regiment to be led by Swiss and German officers and NCOs recruited in continental Europe, the men being enlisted in North America especially from Protestant German and Swiss colonists in Pennsylvania. There was no trouble recruiting Swiss and German cadres in Europe dur-

---

27 Officers
554 NCOs and Men

8 Fusilier Companies
1 Grenadier Company
1 Light Infantry Company

Uniform: red with blue facings. The enlisted men's coats were plain and did not have regimental lace. Officers of the Royal Americans had their uniforms laced with silver.

Officer, Grenadier Company, 60th Foot (Royal Americans), 1755-1767.
(Print after an artist's impression by P.W. Reynolds)

> **2nd BATTALION - 60th FOOT**
> **(THE ROYAL AMERICAN REGIMENT OF FOOT)**
> *Brigadier-General Hon. Robert Monckton*

---

ing 1756 but enlistments in America did not attain the hoped-for levels. By 1757, the 60th had about 1800 Americans, half of them of German origin, after recruiting efforts in Pennsylvania and New York, which was less than half of its allowed establishment. The regiment was finally completed with 3,900 men during that year by massive drafts of recruits. Of these, about half were Irish with a quarter American and a quarter German.

The 1st battalion was led by John Stanwix and, except for five companies detached to Charleston, South Carolina in 1757-1758, served in Pennsylvania and in the Ohio Valley throughout the war.

The 2nd battalion was under the command of Robert Monckton, replaced by James Murray on 24 October 1759. It was in New York until sent to Halifax in 1757 to take part in the planned expedition against Louisbourg. When this was cancelled, the battalion was sent to Philadelphia. It returned to Halifax in 1758 for the fresh attempt on Louisbourg. The 2nd battalion participated in the siege and capture of Louisbourg in June and July and was part of the expedition up the St John River in the fall. Some 591 all ranks from the 2nd battalion embarked for Québec in June 1759.

WOLFE'S COMMAND

3rd BRIGADE

The junior brigadier, who commanded the 3rd Brigade, was James Murray, born in January 1722 at Ballencrief, Scotland, the fifth son of Elizabeth Stirling and Alexander Murray, 4th Baron Elibank. In 1736, he joined as a cadet in Colyear's Regiment, a mercenary corps in the Scottish Brigade in Dutch service stationed at Ypres (Belgium). He transferred to British service in 1740 as second lieutenant in the 4th Marines and was in the failed Cartagena expedition; captain in the 15th Foot the next year; in Flanders in 1745 where he was seriously wounded at Ostend but recovered to take part in the raid against Lorient in 1746.

In 1750, Murray became a major and, the following year, lieutenant-colonel of his 15th Foot. During the Seven Years' War, he participated with his regiment in the abortive Rochefort raid in 1757 and came to North America with the 15th in 1758. He was in Wolfe's brigade at the siege of Louisbourg where he was noted for his distinguished services and great energy. Impressed, Wolfe selected him to be a brigadier in his

> 35th Regiment of Foot
> 48th Regiment of Foot
> 3rd Battalion, 60th Regiment of Foot
> (The Royal American Regiment of Foot)

Québec expedition. But Murray was also very ambitious and it was later said he took the task as a way to get ahead more than for any reciprocal feelings toward Wolfe. And, as the siege went on, Murray was to develop a deep antipathy for his commander.

Like the other two brigades, the 3rd was formed following Wolfe's orders on 4 May. It consisted of Otway's 35th Foot, Webb's 48th Foot and Lawrence's 3rd Battalion of the 60th Foot. Like the first two brigades, Murray's 3rd Brigade practised landings and battlefield deployment at Louisbourg until it sailed with the army for Québec in early June. Once it had reached Québec, the 3rd Brigade was to be used to secure positions west of Point Levy on the south shore but Wolfe soon changed his mind. Instead, Murray joined Townshend's 2nd Brigade at the Montmorency camp from 10 July. At the end of July, the 3rd Brigade detached its grenadier companies to participate in the landings west of the Montmorency falls. The landing was repulsed and the best Murray and his men could do was to try to cover the retreat.

As Murray was the junior brigadier, he was basically under Townshend while posted at Montmorency. On 3 August, Wolfe finally gave him an independent task. He was to bring his troops west of Point Levy on the south shore and board Royal Navy ships to 'try at their (the French) Magazines and Shipping' up river so as to distract and divide the French forces. The 3rd Battalion of the 60th Foot therefore marched up to the Etchemin River and was joined in that area by other troops including some rangers. Webb's 48th was, however, detached to garrison Point Levy. Otway's 35th was left in Montmorency. It seems therefore that the 3rd Brigade

Brigadier-General James Murray, c.1765. After the war Murray remained as governor of Canada, a most delicate post as he had to conciliate the Canadian population to British rule and customs.
(National Archives of Canada, C2834)

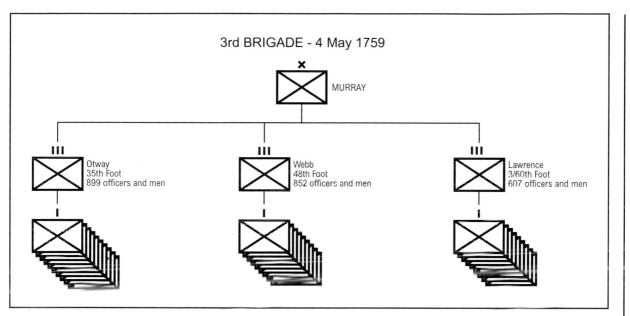

3rd BRIGADE - 4 May 1759

MURRAY

Otway
35th Foot
899 officers and men

Webb
48th Foot
852 officers and men

Lawrence
3/60th Foot
607 officers and men

was split between various places by August. Certainly, it did not act as a brigade at all. Murray's command was therefore a collection of various detachments although the 3rd Battalion of the 60th, or part of the battalion, was the main unit of his force. Still, Murray's wanderings on the river west of the city did draw Montcalm's attention. They had to be constantly watched and a powerful corps under Colonel Bougainville was tasked to follow the British ships in a game of hide and seek that lasted for over a month.

On 8 August, Murray tried to land at Pointe-aux-Trembles. The attempt failed utterly. The first attempt was foiled when the boats ran on to rocks just below the surface. By the time the second attempt was under way, Bougainville and his men were waiting in position and in strength on the north shore. The British were repulsed, having suffered about 110 soldiers and 30 sailors killed or wounded.

Still, Murray was not discouraged and on 18 August, he made a successful landing at Deschambault, a village west of Québec on the north shore. The place was undefended and Murray's men captured spare equipment and supplies stored there for Montcalm's five metropolitan battalions. These were burned as well as whatever else could be destroyed. Some few local militiamen and some Corps of Cavalry troopers came up but were kept a safe distance away by the British troops. The main body of Bougainville's force arrived on the spot at the end of the day. It was too late as the British were back on their ships and Murray was no doubt happy at pulling off a successful raid.

Murray's force west of the city did worry Montcalm as he wondered if the British might not try to establish a permanent position to cut off communications. Wolfe, for his part, was far from happy with Murray's actions. He was hoping his raids would bring out Montcalm for a general action. Instead, he became increasingly upset as he was not getting many reports from Murray and it obviously seemed to Wolfe that nothing much was being done. French ships further west in the St Lawrence River had not been touched either, so the whole operation seemed a failure. On 22 August, an irate Wolfe recalled Murray. Their relations now became quite strained. By now, Wolfe was sick again but had resolved to abandon Montmorency.

The 3rd Brigade had existed only on paper since the beginning of August. On 7 September, it was reformed under Murray's command and made up of the 35th, Anstruther's 58th and the Louisbourg Grenadiers. This structure was not followed, as with any of the brigades at the battle of the Plains, and only the 58th was under Murray while the 35th and the Louisbourg Grenadiers were under Monckton. At 1800 hrs that day, Townshend ordered that the 3rd Brigade be under the command of Lieutenant-Colonel Hunt Walsh of the 28th and made up of the 28th, the 35th and the 47th. It was later dissolved when some of the regiments left Québec in October.

As for James Murray, he stayed the winter of 1759-1760 in Québec as the governor and commander of the garrison. During the summer, Murray cautiously led his forces from Québec to Montréal, one of the three British armies converging on the city which surrendered on 8 September. He was later promoted to lieutenant-general.

35th REGIMENT OF FOOT

The 35th was raised in northern Ireland in 1701. From 26 July 1717 to 10 August 1764, the colonel was General Charles Otway. It was sent to North America in 1756 embarking at Plymouth in April and arriving at Albany, New York, during June. In America, it was led by Lieutenant-Colonel George Monro. From there the 35th proceeded to Fort William-Henry situated at the southern end of Lake George, below Lake Champlain.

Its 600 men were part of the 2,800-strong garrison – 800 regulars and the rest New England provincials – of the fort when General Montcalm laid siege to it with 4,000 French and Canadians and 2,000 Indians. Lieutenant-Colonel Monro commanded the garrison as the French started siege operations on 4 August and the fort surrendered on the 9th after a valiant but hopeless defence. Granted the honours of war, the garrison marched out but, on the way to Fort Edward, was attacked by the Indians who were frustrated by not obtaining booty and prisoners. A massacre ensued, later consideraby magnified by the Anglo-American press, which was stopped by Montcalm's personal intervention with his troops. Still, scores of men were missing not to mention the trauma the incident caused.

The British and New Englanders were, like the men of the 35th, shocked and outraged. Many believed, wrongly as it turned out, that Montcalm had done this on purpose. In the future, their battle cry fighting the French would be 'Remember Fort William-Henry'. Reinforced and reorganised, the 35th was sent to Halifax and 566 all ranks were present at the 1758 siege of Louisbourg. Following the surrender of the fortress, the 35th was transferred to Annapolis Royal in Nova Scotia.

35th REGIMENT OF FOOT
General Charles Otway

In the spring of 1759, the regiment was sent back to Louisbourg to join Wolfe's expedition to Québec. Some 899 officers and men of Otway's 35th Foot embarked at Louisbourg for Québec in June 1759 and 519 were present at the battle of the Plains on 13 September, where they protected the right flank of General Wolfe's main battleline. It faced somewhat obliquely towards the

---

36 Officers
863 NCOs and Men

8 Fusilier Companies
1 Grenadier Company
1 Light Infantry Company

Uniform: red with orange facings, white lace with a black and an orange line and an orange zigzag between, pewter buttons.
Silver buttons and lace for officers.

---

left flank of the French line which included Canadian militias and the Royal-Roussillon Regiment. Many popular British accounts of the battle have repeated that Royal-Roussillon was the 35th of the French line infantry. However, the French army lists – the yearly 'Etat militaire de France' – show it to be the 37th Regiment. In any case, the 35th, led by Lieutenant-Colonel Henry Fletcher, charged and routed the French troops facing them.

Regimental legend has it that the 35th captured a colour of the Royal-Roussillon Regiment and also took white plumes from its grenadiers. This is possible but period evidence or trophies to confirm the story do not seem to have survived.

Another mystery concerning the 35th is the unidentified figure of a grenadier at the right of Benjamin West's famous 1770 painting of the Death of Wolfe. He is dressed in the red uniform with orange facings of the 35th which seems to indicate he was with the regiment. Inspection returns of May and June 1768 mention black gaiters with white garters for the regiment, the same as in the picture. One presumes he paid the £100 West is said to have asked to be included in the painting.

The 35th remained in Canada and was at the surrender of Montréal in 1760. In 1762 it participated in the capture of Martinique and Havana in the Carribean. It was posted to Pensacola, Florida from 1763 until it finally returned to Britain in 1765.

48th REGIMENT OF FOOT

The regiment was originally raised in 1740 but was renumbered 48th in 1748. It served in Flanders and Scotland during the 1740s. From April 1752 to 11 November 1755, the regiment's colonel was Thomas Dunbar and thereafter until December 1766, the colonel was Lieutenant-General Daniel Webb. Following the Jumonville incident in the Ohio Valley, the 48th was sent to North America with the 44th to reinforce the American colonies which then had very few regular British troops for their defence against the French and Indians. General Edward Braddock was sent to command the troops whose mission it was to expel the French from the Ohio valley where they had built a number of forts. The 48th arrived with the 44th at Alexandria, Virginia, in 1755. It was part of General Braddock's army defeated by the French and Indians at the Monongahela in July. During the battle, General Braddock was killed. Colonel Dunbar took a leading part in saving what was left of the Anglo-American army from the enemy.

48th REGIMENT OF FOOT
Lieutenant-General Daniel Webb

Reorganised in Pennsylvania and New York in 1756–1757, the 48th spent the winter of 1757–1758 in New York and was then sent to Halifax where General Amherst's army was gathering to attack Fortress Louisbourg. 928 officers and men participated in the 1758 siege of Louisbourg.

Following the capture of Louisbourg, the 48th was sent back to New England and spent the winter of 1758-1759 quartered in Connecticut. In the spring of 1759, Webb's 48th was back at Louisbourg in order to join the army of General Wolfe being assembled for the expedition to Québec. Some 852 officers and men of the 48th embarked aboard Admiral Saunders' fleet in June and 683 were present at the battle of the Plains on 13 September, forming Wolfe's reserve.

The 48th was one of the regiments left to garrison Québec with the force under General Murray. It was engaged in further fighting against the French under General Lévis during the following year which culminated with the surrender of Montréal on 8 September 1760. Canada was now under British rule

---

36 Officers
816 NCOs and Men

8 Fusilier Companies
1 Grenadier Company
1 Light Infantry Company

Uniform: red with buff facings, white lace with green and yellow lines, pewter buttons.
Gold buttons and lace for officers.

---

and the 48th was one of the units selected to remain in garrison.

It was assigned to the area of Trois-Rivières. But in June 1761, the 48th was ordered to New York and sailed for the West Indies in November as part of General Burton's force. In 1762, it was part of the army under Lord Rollo that took Martinique from the French and Havana from the Spanish. The 48th finally returned to Britain in 1763.

Grenadier, Webb's 48th Foot, 1750s.
(Watercolour by Cecil C.P. Lawson after David Morier. Anne S.K. Brown Military Collection, Brown University. Photo R. Chartrand)

3rd Battalion – 60th FOOT
(THE ROYAL AMERICAN REGIMENT OF FOOT)

The 3rd battalion of the 60th Royal Americans was raised from January 1756. From February 1757, it was led by Charles Lawrence. It was posted from Albany to south of Lake Champlain in 1757. In early August, a 100-man detachment was sent to reinforce Fort William-Henry. This was an unlucky posting as the fort was besieged by General Montcalm from 4 to 9 August when it surrendered.

> ### 2nd BATTALION - 60th FOOT
> ### (THE ROYAL AMERICAN REGIMENT OF FOOT)
> *Brigadier-General Charles Lawrence*

In October, the remainder of 3/60th, which had been with other troops at Fort Edward, was transferred to Nova Scotia. It took its winter quarters at Dartmouth, near Halifax. The battalion was to be part of General Amherst's force of 12,000 men which was assembling at Halifax to board Admiral Boscawen's fleet. The army's objective was the French fortress of Louisbourg. About 800 strong, the 3rd battalion of the 60th landed on Cape Breton Island in early June. The 3/60th was part of the 1st Brigade under Brigadier-General Whitmore. Along with other units in the army, its men took part in the elaborate siege operations which led to the capture of Louisbourg on 26 July. Following the siege, the 3/60th went back to Halifax where it spent the winter.

Having been selected as one of the units to take part in General Wolfe's expedition against Québec, the 3/60th went back in May 1759 to Louisbourg where the army was assembling. Some 607 all ranks embarked at Louisbourg on board Admiral Saunders' fleet which sailed in June 1759. The 3/60th played a distinguished part in the siege and capture of Québec. In August, the battalion was part of Murray's force of about 1,200 men which raided Deschambault west of Québec. It went up to the Plains on 13 September. Initially the battalion was employed protecting Wolfe's left flank but later in the action it was pulled back to cover the landing site at the Anse-au-Foulon. After the war it went on to serve in the West Indies and was disbanded during 1764.

This account of the 60th would not be complete without mentioning the 4th battalion. In 1757, it was

> 29 Officers
> 578 NCOs and Men
>
> 8 Fusilier Companies
> 1 Grenadier Company
> 1 Light Infantry Company
>
> Uniform: red with blue facings. The enlisted men's coats were plain and did not have regimental lace.
> Officers of the Royal Americans had their uniforms laced with silver.

Private, 60th Foot (Royal Americans), 1755-1767. (Print after an artist's impression by P.W. Reynolds)

sent from New York to Halifax to participate in the Louisbourg expedition. When the expedition was cancelled, the battalion was sent back to New York and, in 1758, was part of General James Abercromby's army defeated by Montcalm at Ticonderoga on 8 July. The following year, the 4th/60th took part in the siege and capture of Fort Niagara and the capture of Montréal in 1760, where it remained until it was disbanded in 1763.

ROYAL ARTILLERY

From the late 17th century, the Board of Ordnance maintained detachments of regular gunners in Newfoundland, and in Nova Scotia from 1710. In the 1720s, the detachments were amalgamated into the newly-formed Royal Regiment of Artillery, better known as the Royal Artillery.

A relatively small corps at its beginning, it was nevertheless notable for its good organisation, matériel and training. Its expertise in both theory and practice as well as the resilience and good service given by British gunners on the battlefield earned the Royal Artillery an enviable reputation as one of the better artillery corps. The field guns served by the officers and men of the regiment in the middle of the 18th century were usually 6-pounders, but also included the heavier 9- and 12-pounders. There were also 10- and 12-inch howitzers and heavier siege artillery. Each company of the Royal Artillery had a proportion of bombardiers who were gunners with greater skills for they served the dangerous and complicated mortars.

> ROYAL ARTILLERY
> *Lieutenant-Colonel George Williamson*

Officer, Royal Artillery in campaign dress, late 1750s – early 1760s.
(Print after R.J. Macdonald based on contemporary portraits)

---

21 Officers
309 NCOs and Men

3 Companies

Uniform: blue with red facings, yellow lace and brass buttons.
Gold buttons and lace for officers.

At the outbreak of the Seven Years' War, there were only two companies of the Royal Artillery in North America but this was doubled in 1757, two more companies being sent in 1758. Detachments served on the various fronts and were present in all major engagements. As operations became larger and required more siege artillery, the personnel of the Royal Artillery involved were more numerous. Three companies amounting to 330 officers and men took part in the siege of Louisbourg in June and July 1758, an operation which required considerable artillery to bombard the town into surrendering.

By 1759, the regiment had grown to 24 companies of which eight were now posted in North America. Three companies totalling 330 officers and men embarked at Louisbourg for Québec in June 1759. They were under the command of Lieutenant-Colonel George Williamson. Their most valuable contribution was the relentless service of the heavy guns and mortars installed in the batteries set up on Point Levy which, from 12 July to 12 September, destroyed part of the city by bombardment.

At the battle of the Plains on 13 September, the Royal Artillery had six officers with 40 artillerymen manning three field pieces. Following the fall of Québec, two companies of the Royal Artillery were left with General Murray's forces.

With Montréal remaining as the final French stronghold in Canada, in 1760 they joined five more artillery companies who were with the British and New England forces which were converging on the city.

Following the surrender of Montréal, and the fall of New France, most companies went on to campaign against the French and Spanish in the West Indies.

LOUISBOURG GRENADIERS

On 30 May 1759, the grenadier companies of the 22nd (Whitmore's), 40th (Hopson's) and the 45th (Warburton's) garrisoned at Louisbourg were assembled into a temporary elite formation by General Wolfe and named the 'Louisbourg Grenadiers'. Wolfe needed all the elite shock troops he could get and wasted no time in incorporating the Louisbourg Grenadiers into his army. There were 326 of all ranks.

> **LOUISBOURG GRENADIERS**
> *Lieutenant-Colonel Alexander Murray*

Two of the three regiments from which the companies were detached had long service in North America. From independent companies already posted in those colonies, Hopson's 40th was formed in Nova Scotia and Newfoundland in 1717. The unit remained in Nova Scotia and Newfoundland, as Britain and especially New England became increasingly worried about the construction of the French fortress town at

Grenadier, Warburton's 45th Foot.

(Anne S.K. Brown Military Collection, Brown University. Photo R. Chartrand)

---

13 Officers
313 NCOs and Men

1 Company from the 22nd Regiment of Foot
Lieutenant-General Edward Whitmore
108 officers, NCOs and men
Uniform: red with pale buff facings, white lace with two red and blue lines, pewter buttons, mitre grenadier caps.
Silver buttons and lace for officers.

1 Company from the 40th Regiment of Foot
Lieutenant-General Thomas Hopson/
Lieutenant-General John Barrington
110 officers, NCOs and men
Uniform: red with buff facings, white lace with a black line edged buff, pewter buttons, mitre grenadier caps.
Gold buttons and lace for officers.

1 Company from the 45th Regiment of Foot
General Hugh Warburton
108 officers, NCOs and men
Uniform: red with green facings, white lace with a green line and green stars, pewter buttons, mitre grenadier caps.
Silver buttons and lace for officers.

Louisbourg. From 4 March 1752 to 9 June 1759, its colonel was Lieutenant-General Thomas Hopson who was succeeded by John Barrington.

The 45th had been sent to reinforce the garrison of Nova Scotia in 1746 and had taken part in the 1758 capture of Louisbourg.

The 22nd arrived at Halifax during 1756. It participated in the siege of Louisbourg in 1758 where it remained as part of the garrison.

During the campaign, the unit was often in service near Wolfe's HQ. Some 80 men from each company were present at the battle of the Plains. The companies remained in the city until late October when they returned to their respective units thus ending the short existence of one of the most celebrated temporary units in the history of the British Army.

LIGHT INFANTRY

Following Braddock's disaster on the Monongahela and the failure of Sir William Johnson to follow up his victory over Dieskau at Lake George by a pursuit into the wilderness, it was clear to the British High Command that light troops would be needed to break the Canadian and Indian domination of the forests as tactical ground. When Lord Loudoun arrived in North

---

LIGHT INFANTRY

Lieutenant-Colonel William Howe

Major John Dalling

America as commander-in-chief, he instantly saw that no strategic advances could be made without strong bodies of light infantry to precede the large contingents of line infantry necessary to mount a successful invasion of New France. Loudoun noted the value of the New England Rangers and encouraged Robert Rogers and Joseph Goreham to raise additional companies. But Loudoun as well as his successors, generals Abercromby and Amherst, wished to have a better disciplined force than the somewhat unruly and independently-minded rangers. Thus, when Lieutenant-Colonel Thomas Gage, 44th Foot, proposed to raise a regular regiment of light infantry, Loudoun approved and the 80th 'Light Armed Foot' was added to the rolls of the regular army in 1758. It was raised in America, dressed in brown uniforms, armed with light muskets and served in the Lake Champlain area.

More regular light infantry was needed quickly and, in early 1758, Major George Scott, 40th Foot, who was

Lieutenant-Colonel William Howe. He commanded the Light Infantry and Rangers during the siege of Québec. This miniature is said to have belonged to General Wolfe.
(National Archives of Canada, C96944)

---

11 Officers
About 300 NCOs and Men

3 Companies of 'well-chosen men' with a subaltern and a sergeant detached from the Light Infantry of each regiment.

Uniform: the regimentals of the various detachments forming the light infantry were altered according to Wolfe's order of 30 May 1759 which specified 'the sleeves of the coat are put on the waist coat, and instead of coat sleeves he has two wings like the Grenadiers but fuller' the regimental lace taken off but the lapels kept; the coat tails were cut short; the tricorn hat 'made into a cap with a flap and button and with as much black cloth added as will come under his chin ...it hooks in the front, and is made like the old velvet caps of England'.

---

familiar with irregular tactics, raised a corps of light infantry drawn from detachments of officers and men from each regular line regiment of the expedition to capture Fortress Louisbourg. They formed, according to a witness, 'a Corps of 550 Volunteers chosen as Marksmen out of the most active resolute Men from all the Battalions of Regulars.' After giving good service during the siege operations, some were detached with rangers in the fall of 1758 to provide light infantry cover for the troops moving up the St. John River. On 23 November, the corps was dissolved and the men went back to their respective units.

General Wolfe had noted the important services of these troops in the 1758 campaign. It was important that his army for Québec should have a strong, important body of regulars as light infantry. Thus, he gave orders at Halifax in May 1759 for the formation of a corps of light infantry under Lieutenant-Colonel William Howe. The strength of this corps during the siege of Québec is open to conjecture, various records giving anywhere from two to six hundred men. This was probably due to counting the rangers and/or additional troops attached to the light infantry later during the siege.

NEW ENGLAND RANGERS

Units of men patroling the nearby forests to provide some protection against raids on the villages of New England had existed since the 17th century. They were called 'rangers' and gathered the militiamen more adept to woodcraft which were relatively few, the British colonies being much more oriented towards agriculture and the sea than to roaming in the wilderness. While there were some notable exceptions previously, it was really during the Seven Years' War that rangers truly became important tactical entities serving as permanent troops with the regular armies. Much of this was due to Joseph Goreham who raised the first truly regular ranger units for service in Nova Scotia in the 1740s and to Robert Rogers who raised ranger companies to scout the Lake Champlain area from 1755. A powerful boost to the concept of bush warfare practised by rangers was the enthusiastic support of Lord Loudoun who perceived that these tactics, allied with the new light infantry tactics and units, could provide the early warning 'screen' and information needed by conventional armies campaigning in North America. Companies of rangers were thus found on all fronts.

NEW ENGLAND RANGERS
Major George Scott

For the Québec expedition, Wolfe needed some 600 rangers with his army besides light infantry, a reasonable number considering he would be in the heart of French Canada and would have to control the countryside adjacent to his army. Five companies embarked at Louisbourg in June 1759 on the fleet sailing to Québec. Benonie Dank's company joined the expedition at Bird Island. The six companies of New England Rangers totalled 576 officers and men. They were commanded by Major George Scott, 40th Foot. The six companies of rangers were the first troops to land on Ile d'Orléans on 25 June and had the first skirmish of the campaign there. A few days later, they helped take Point Levy. Two companies of rangers were part of the force that secured the east shore of the Montmorency River in early July, others participating in raids west of Québec. The destruction of villages ordered by Wolfe in August was largely performed by the rangers and could be quite

24 Officers
546 NCOs and Men

Jonathan Brewer's Company
3 Officers and 82 NCOs and men
Benonie Dank's Company
3 Officers and 90 NCOs and men
Joseph Goreham's (also spelt Gorham's) Company
7 Officers and 88 NCOs and men
Moses Hazen's Company
3 Officers and 86 NCOs and men
James Rogers' Company
4 Officers and 108 NCOs and men
William Starks' Company
3 Officers and 92 NCOs and men

Uniform: in May 1759, Captain Knox noted that 'The rangers have got a new uniform clothing, the ground is of black ratteen of frize, lapelled and cuffed in blue, here follows a description of their dress; a waistcoat with sleeves; a short jacket without sleeves; only armholes and wings to the shoulders (in like manner as the Grenadiers and drummers of the army) white metal buttons, canvas drawers, with a blue skirt or petticoat of stuff, made with a waistband and one button; this open before and does not quite extend to their knees, a pair of leggings of the same color with their coat, which reach up to the middle of the thighs (without flaps) and from the calf of the leg downward they button like spatter-dashes; with this active dress they wear blue bonnets, and I think, in great measure resemble our Highlanders'.

challenging at times. At Baie Saint-Paul on 7 August for instance, Goreham's company with 40 other troops had a sharp two-hour fight before defeating the local inhabitants and putting the village to the torch. Because Scott and most of his men were detached in various places, the rangers did not participate in the battle of the Plains. Following the surrender of Québec, Hazen's Company remained in the city with Murray's army while the five other companies returned to New England.

COLONIAL PIONEERS

The British forces involved in the 1759 siege of Québec were notable in that there were very few American troops with Wolfe's army. There were only the six companies of rangers whose participation was noted in many accounts and the pioneers described below. This was a considerable change from the British armies on Lake Champlain and in the Ohio Valley which each had thousands of American 'provincial' troops in their ranks. Some of these units, such as George Washington's Virginia Regiment, were considered nearly as good as British regular troops. American troops were raised seasonally, often for eight month periods, by their own provincial legislatures and were paid and supplied by their respective colonies. Massachusetts having the largest population enlisted the largest number of men in its provincial forces; some 6,800 in 1759. This, however, often did not include additional companies of rangers, artisans and bateaux-men paid by the British treasury as well as sailors on provincial gunboats.

Such was the case for the almost unknown corps pioneers which were requested in May by a letter from Wolfe to the Lieutenant-Governor of Massachusetts. The colony agreed and some 300 Massachusetts militiamen were enlisted to serve with the Québec expedition. In July 1759, the pioneers for the expedition arrived from Boston and joined the army besieging Québec. They do not seem to have been enlisted as primarily fighting military men, but as a mostly non-combatant pioneer corps. However some appear to have volunteered for more action by transferring to the rangers who needed reinforcements. Such was the case of pioneer Jeremiah Pearson of Newbury Falls, Massachusetts, who became a ranger in Captain Hazen's company of rangers.

Most, and perhaps nearly all, the men of the pioneer corps' companies appear to have been enlisted in Massachusetts. They would have been used to construct and/or maintain the various field fortifications, batteries and camps of the British forces during the siege. Captain Knox mentioned that some were posted on Île d'Orléans shortly after their arrival. The pioneers did not participate in the battles of Montmorency or of the Plains of Abraham. Nothing is currently known of their equipment, arms and uniforms if they had any. Following the capture of Québec the Massachusetts pioneers sailed back to Boston and were probably disbanded on arrival.

A model of Québec built by the Royal Engineers between 1806 and 1810. The engineers frequently constructed such elaborate three-dimensional models, particularly when planning defences or preparing for siege operations.

THE ROYAL NAVY

THE QUÉBEC EXPEDITION FLEET

Voltaire wrote 'In this country (England), it is useful to kill an Admiral now and then, just to encourage the others'. The great French philosopher and wit was referring to the execution of Admiral Byng who had been made the scapegoat and executed for the loss of Minorca to the French in 1756. Whether Byng should have been put in front of a firing squad is debatable but, although brave, he was indeed none too keen on engaging the enemy.

Certainly, for the Royal Navy, the message was clear: daring and efficiency were the pre-eminent qualities required of an officer. Of course, high birth and patronage could help one's career but it would not excuse incompetence, as the fate of Byng, who was the

Admiral Sir Charles Saunders.

(Print after Sir Joshua Reynolds' 1765 portrait)

fourth son of Viscount Torrington, proved. Sir Edward Hawke, who succeeded Byng, was far more typical of the efficiency of the British naval officer corps. Putting to good use their superiority in numbers, they soon turned the tables and, with increasing efficiency, blockaded the French fleet in its home ports.

In 1757, a strong French squadron had been able to roam the North Atlantic, anchoring at Louisbourg and foiling any chance of success for Lord Loudoun's planned attack on the fortress. But, by the next year, with the reinforced blockade around the coast of France, no fleet came out and Louisbourg was taken.

> *Vice-Admiral Charles Saunders*
> Senior Naval Officer
>
> *Rear-Admiral Philip Durell*
> 2nd-in-Command
>
> *Rear-Admiral Charles Holmes*
> 3rd-in-Command

By 1759, following Hawke's brilliant victory over the French fleet at Quiberon Bay, Britain's naval superiority ensured that a large part of the fleet could go to Québec.

The organisation of the Royal Navy went, very broadly, according to 1731 King's Regulations and Admiralty Instructions which called for nine 'flag officers' or admirals, three to each of the three existing squadrons. The senior admiral was to command the red squadron of the centre, so called because it hoisted red ensigns, the other squadrons being the white and the blue. This simple organisation was not too flexible on paper and, in 1747, when new admirals were appointed, wags in London soon spoke of the non-existent 'Yellow Squadron' to accommodate retiring flag officers. In fact, jokes apart, such appointments increased flexibility and efficiency, the composition of fleets being ultimately subject to practical objectives rather than theoretical practices. A good example is the composition of Hawke's fleet at Quiberon, which comprised larger vessels to face the French battle fleet, while the Québec fleet had ships more suitable for a siege and inshore work.

The commander of the Québec Expedition Fleet, Sir Charles Saunders, had been chosen by William Pitt and Admiral Sir George Anson, whose protégé he was. Having been Comptroller of the Navy as well as an experienced sailor and fighting officer, Saunders combined all the qualities required of the commander of the fleet bound for Québec. The treacherous St Lawrence required a prudent and determined sailor.

To coordinate efficiently the needs and objectives of the thousands of officers and soldiers of Wolfe's army required a skilled and experienced senior administrator, and, with an objective such as Québec, an experienced fighting man was essential.

As second-in-command, Saunders chose Rear-Admiral Philip Durell who was experienced in North American waters while his third-in-command was Rear-Admiral Charles Holmes, who had distinguished himself in operations in the North Sea.

Admiral Durrell was ordered to lead with a vanguard of ten warships and three transports which sailed from Halifax on 5 May. The rest of the fleet assembled at Louisbourg and was divided into three divisions These equated to each of the army's brigades: the White Division 1st brigade, the 2nd brigade – the Red Division – while the 3rd brigade was the Blue Division,

Edward Hughes, captain of HMS *Somerset* at the siege of Québec, who became famous for his battles in the Indian Ocean in the 1770s.
(1803 print after Sir Joshua Reynolds. National Archives of Canada, C8561)

Up until the middle of the 18th century, Britain did not have a permanent corps of marines for its warships. Sea-soldiers tended to be raised in regiments that were raised during wartime and disbanded or incorporated into the land forces when peace was at hand. In the 1740s, for example, ten marine regiments had been

---

SHIPS SAILING TO QUÉBEC FROM LOUISBOURG ON 4th JUNE 1759
Total of fleet: 141 vessels manned by about 13,000 sailors.

HMS *Neptune* 90 guns
HMS *Princess Amelia* 80
HMS *Royal William* 84
HMS *Dublin* 74
HMS *Vanguard* 74
HMS *Terrible* 74
HMS *Shrewsbury* 74
HMS *Devonshire* 74
HMS *Captain* 70
HMS *Bedford* 68
HMS *Northumberland* 64
HMS *Orford* 64
HMS *Prince Frederick* 64
HMS *Alcide* 64
HMS *Stirling Castle* 64
HMS *Centurion* 60
HMS *Pembroke* 60
HMS *Prince of Orange* 60
HMS *Medway* 60
HMS *Trident* 54
HMS *Sutherland* 50

Frigates:
HMS *Diana* 36
HMS *Richmond* 32
HMS *Trent* 28
HMS *Lowestoft* 28
HMS *Echo* 24

Sloops:
HMS *Lizard* 28
HMS *Eurus* 22
HMS *Nightingale* 20
HMS *Hind* 20
HMS *Squirrel* 20
HMS *Scarborough* 20
HMS *Scorpion* 14
HMS *Zephir* 12
HMS *Hunter* 10
HMS *Baltimore* 10
HMS *Cormorant* 8
HMS *Pelican* 8
HMS *Racehorse* 8
HMS *Bonetta* 8
HMS *Strombolo*
HMS *Vesuvius*
HMS *Rodney* 2 (cutter)

34 English transport ships
7 English ordnance vessels
4 English victuallers' vessels
6 American ordnance vessels
68 American transport ships, including sloops and schooners

Private, Royal Marines, 1750s.

ROYAL MARINE BATTALION
Major Boisrond

25 Officers
577 NCO's and marines

Uniform: red with white facings, white lace with a dark blue line or blue and red lace, pewter buttons, mitre grenadier caps.
Gold buttons and lace for officers.

raised. Young James Wolfe had his first commission in his father's 1st Marine Regiment which was disbanded with the other regiments in 1748.

Therefore, in 1755, on the verge of the outbreak of the Seven Years' War, Britain once again raised a body of sea-soldiers to garrison its warships. The new organisation was different. Instead of regiments, the new corps was made up of 50 independent companies divided into three divisions, one at each of Britain's great naval bases: Portsmouth, Plymouth and Chatham. The HQ for each division detached a number of marines

from its companies to serve on board the warships sailing from that port. For expeditions, temporary battalions could be formed. Instead of tricorn hats, the marines wore the mitre-shaped grenadier caps of elite troops.

During the siege of Louisbourg, some 500 marines were landed on 25 June and were posted at Kensington Cove in Gabarus Bay west of the fortress. Another 100 were landed on 2 July to join Wolfe's brigade. At Wolfe's request, these marines wore instead of their uniform 'cropped hats, shot jackets, etc., thirty-six rounds of ammunition, and a blanket [to] each man rolled up on their back.' Most marines served with the artillery during the siege.

The marine contingent present at the siege of Québec is usually not recorded in most accounts, as they were not part of the army's land forces. Some 1,200 marines – and possibly more – served on land during the siege. A special temporary battalion was detached from Portsmouth to take part in the expedition. They were posted with the artillery batteries at Point Levy, with two companies reinforcing Wolfe's camp at Montmorency from 26 July. By the end of August, nearly 1,100 marines were at Point Levy. Another 600 marines were landed from the ships at the Ile d'Orléans in late July. In all likelihood, there were also several hundred more marines still serving on board the warships.

The marines did not participate in the battle of the Plains. However, while the real attack was taking place, warships made a demonstration for a mock attack east of the city, got as close to shore as they could, filled boats with marines and lowered them to deceive the French into expecting a landing there.

A sailor, from one of the Royal Navy's numerous warships operating in the St Lawrence, with two British soldiers in Québec.
(Detail from a print after Richard Short. National Archives of Canada, C351)

PRELIMINARIES
26th June – 28th June 1759

Descent on Québec

The army assembled at Louisbourg to perform the task was smaller than had been originally planned by Pitt. Instead of 12,000 men, there were only some 8,500 men but it was an excellent force. There were ten battalions of regular line infantry, a small three-company elite battalion called the 'Louisbourg Grenadiers' and three companies of the Royal Artillery. All these were British regular troops and the only New Englanders were six companies of rangers. Not usually accounted for was a battalion of marines and the marines on board the warships. The expedition was later joined by 300 New England pioneers so that the total figure actually came to about 10,000 men. A corps of light infantry was drawn from the various regular British regiments to act as skirmishers. Its exact numbers are somewhat vague as they were accounted for within the ten battalions. At times it would also include the 300 rangers in a group as large as 600 men. In any event, Wolfe deemed he had enough men to carry on. Time was of the essence for an expedition to take Québec. Earlier attempts had failed partly because they started much too late. This time, preparations were completed by the beginning of June. It was a first measure of success.

The fleet assembled at Louisbourg which sailed in early June to transport the force to Québec was truly grand. It consisted of some 49 Royal Navy warships under Admiral Charles Saunders whose flag-ship was the 90-gun HMS *Neptune*. Of these, 22 were ships-of-the-line having 50 guns or more. Besides Saunders' flagship, there were two other three-deck ships, HMS *Princess Amelia* of 80 guns and HMS *Royal William* of 84 guns. It was a larger number of Royal Navy ships than Admiral Sir Edward Hawke was to have at Quiberon, later in 1759, where he vanquished the French fleet although Hawke's ships had more guns than Saunders'. Still, the warships in the fleet sailing

Captain James Cook, master of HMS *Pembroke*, was one of the naval officers responsible for navigating the British fleet throught the difficult waters of the St Lawrence River to Québec.
(Print after N. Dance's 1776 portrait)

towards Québec amounted to about a quarter of the strength of the Royal Navy, a considerable gathering under any circumstances. One of these warships, the 60-gun HMS *Centurion* had an exceptional history for it had been part of Admiral Anson's famous cruise around the world between 1740 and 1744. Admiral Saunders was an accomplished sailor and had been in the crew of the *Centurion* during that cruise. Nor was Saunders the only exceptional sailor in the fleet. James Cook, the celebrated future explorer of the South Pacific, was master on board HMS *Pembroke*. Edward Hughes who would at a future date lock horns with the brilliant Suffren in the Indian Ocean, was captain of HMS *Somerset*. And, commanding the small HMS *Porcupine* was young John Jervis, the future Lord St Vincent. With the warships were some 119 transport ships for troops, ammunition and supplies.

The issue of obtaining good pilots was addressed early for this expedition. It had been one of the major problems for the previous attempts and a solution was vital to success. The British sought French pilots with experience of the St Lawrence among the prisoners they already held. A Canadian captain was found, Denys de Vitré, who had been captured on his frigate, the

26/6/1759	3/7	10/7	14/7	21/7	28/7	4/8	11/8	18/8	25/8	1/9	8/9	12/9	13/9(0400hrs)	(0700hrs)	(0830hrs)	(1000hrs)	(1130hrs)
pages 68-69			70-74		75-77			78-80			81-83			84-91			92-95	

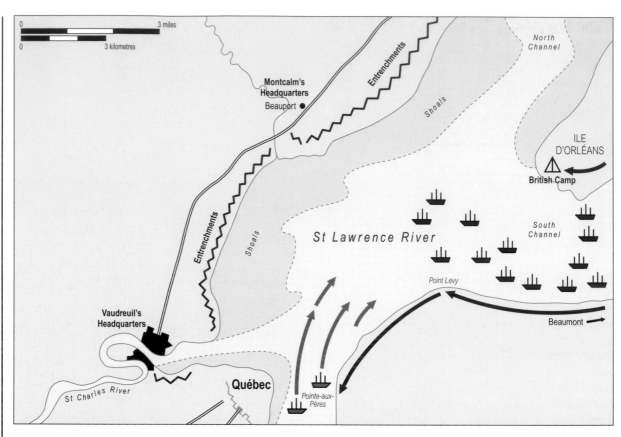

On 27 June the British landed at Beaumont to the east of Québec before advancing to Point Levy. They also landed on Ile d'Orléans and set up a fortified camp. The next night the French sent their fire ships.

32-gun *Renomée*, in 1757. He was brought to Admiral Saunders who, it seems, asked him to choose between a rich reward if he guided the fleet or to be hanged from the nearest mast if he refused. He gave in to the threat and was assigned to pilot Durrell's vanguard. Two other Canadians, Martin Dechenique and Augustin Raby, were pilots on HMS *Neptune* to guide the fleet under threat of being killed according to Captain Knox's journal. The use of death threats on helpless prisoners was an unconscionable act and an odious form of blackmail. Its use, albeit rather sparingly, demonstrates Wolfe's and Saunders' determination to succeed without too much regard for moral niceties.

From late May, Rear-Admiral Philip Durrell, Saunder's second in command was already in the area of Le Bic with his squadron of 10 warships and three transport vessels, narrowly missing a group of 17 French supply ships which reached Québec. As Saunders' fleet came up, Durrell's squadron assumed the role of the vanguard. Other vessels joined as the fleet progressed until there were about 200 ships manned by about 13,000 sailors entering the gulf of the St Lawrence River.

Until this point the French had been able to offer little resistance to the British invasion fleet. Some areas, such as Ile d'Orléans and the south shore to the east were indefensible. On the other hand, the north shore was quite well defended as Wolfe and Mackellar could appreciate. Montcalm had wisely directed many batteries to be built all along the Beauport shore and he himself had set up his HQ in that area. The first response from the French, following the arrival of the British fleet, was to try to set it aflame with fire ships. For weeks, seven ships had been prepared for the task, at great cost it was said. Navy captain Delouche was selected by Vaudreuil for the task although there were several other naval officers senior to him who were anxious for the chance which resulted in some

26/6/1759	3/7	10/7	14/7	21/7	28/7	4/8	11/8	18/8	25/8	1/9	8/9	12/9	13/9(0400hrs)	(0700hrs)	(0830hrs)	(1000hrs)	(1130hrs)
	pages 68-69		70-74		75-77			78-80			81-83			84-91			92-95

The French fire ships drifting down towards the British fleet on the night of 28 June 1759. Note the longboats from the British ships going out to meet them.
(Painting by Doninic Seeres. National Archives of Canada, C4292)

barely out of artillery range when Captain Delouche ordered the ships set ablaze, prematurely as it turned out. The men on the British ships suddenly saw walls of fire drifting towards them. But they were still some distance away and the British sailors manoeuvred the ships nearest to the fire ships out of the way by weighing anchor. HMS *Centurion*, most at risk, simply cut her cables as there was no time to bring up her anchors. Meanwhile, longboats manned by sailors from other British ships rowed towards the fire ships. They grappled the flaming vessels and towed them out of harm's way. The first major French action against the British fleet had failed utterly.

It did create excitement for spectators on both sides. Many people in Québec City were no doubt hoping and praying, for an even bigger blaze including all the British ships on the river but they were soon disappointed. On the British side, the flames and noise at first frightened the soldiers in outposts on Ile d'Orléans. They sounded a general alarm which caused great consternation. Once it had been established that this was not an all-out French attack but an attempt with fire ships, most soldiers went down to the shore to watch the show on the river.

grumbling. Events were to prove the critics of Captain Delouche correct.

On the night of 28 June, seven ships loaded with inflammable materials slid out of Québec drifting, undetected, towards the British ships. But they were

The fire ships being dragged away and beached by sailors in longboats.
(Painting by Doninic Seeres. National Archives of Canada, C4291)

26/6/1759	3/7	10/7	14/7	21/7	28/7	4/8	11/8	18/8	25/8	1/9	8/9	12/9	13/9(0400hrs)	(0700hrs)	(0830hrs)	(1000hrs)	(1130hrs)
	pages 68-69		70-74		75-77			78-80		81-83			84-91			92-95	

PRELIMINARIES
July – August 1759

The Siege of Québec

From his initial survey of the French positions, Wolfe had seen that it would be possible to occupy the heights at Point Levy, right across from the city of Québec. The south shore did not seem to be fortified for a defence and he quickly instructed Brigadier Monckton to move in with his brigade. On the evening of 29 June, a party of light infantry and rangers climbed up the hill and occupied the church at the village of Beaumont. They were joined by the rest of the brigade early the next morning. At that time, the British skirmishers ran into a small party of Canadian militiamen who beat a hurried retreat as they saw numerous redcoats coming after them. The New England Rangers returned from the skirmish with six scalps, to the horror of the British soldiers who were not familiar with the cruder practices of back-woods warfare. They had been led to believe that only the Indians and some Canadian woodsmen carried out this horrible practice. Now they could see it was also done on their side too...

At about noon, Monckton left 250 men at Beaumont and marched the rest of his brigade up to the heights of Point Levy. But as they neared the spot, a party of about 200 Indians and 40 Canadian militiamen from nearby Lauzon under militia captain Charest opened fire on the British troops. Charest sent word for reinforcements from Québec City to keep the enemy off the heights but

Monckton erected his camp at Point Levy and the British batteries were installed at Pointe-aux-Pères. The whole area was often simply called Point Levy.

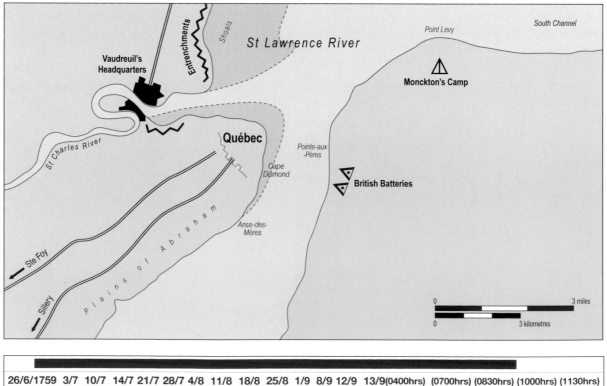

26/6/1759	3/7	10/7	14/7	21/7	28/7	4/8	11/8	18/8	25/8	1/9	8/9	12/9	13/9(0400hrs)	(0700hrs)	(0830hrs)	(1000hrs)	(1130hrs)
pages 65-67			70-74		75-77			78-80			81-83			84-91			92-95

A general view of Québec from Point Levy, c.1759-1760. Montcalm's failure to secure these commanding heights enabled the British to shell the town virtually unopposed.
(Print after Richard Short. National Archives of Canada, C355)

the senior commanders, believing a British deserter, thought it was a feint for an attack on Beauport and sent reinforcements there instead. After three hours of courageous fighting the Indians and militiamen withdrew as they were about to be outflanked by the British.

Wolfe now ordered Guy Carleton to set up a fortified camp on Ile d'Orléans and then went to reconnoitre the heights of Point Levy. From up there, he had a good view of the extensive fortifications of the Beauport shore. It was a disappointment as the works were obviously very strong and would be next to impossible to storm. On the other hand Wolfe, his engineers and especially his artillery officers, as they were looking with their telescopes at the city across the river, realised that, from the height of Point Levy, it lay within artillery range. It was the first major break for the British and batteries for heavy guns were immediately ordered to be built.

Soon, hundreds of men were toiling to set up the batteries and haul the guns up. The Royal Artillery personnel were there too, planning how to best install the heavy guns and mortars. About a mile separated the two shores and, as these experienced gunners and bombardiers knew, from this range they could pour a devastating fire on the lower town in particular.

The French tried to hamper the work of the British with artillery fire from floating and shore batteries. But their cannon balls and shells were largely ineffectual as the French gunners found it difficult to find the range and acquire targets that were usually higher. But perhaps their greatest disadvantage and frustration was that their supply of gunpowder was limited and had to be used sparingly. Thus, some forty British heavy guns and mortars were in position by 12 July. A strong redoubt was also built on the land side by Lieutenant-Colonel Burton's battalion to protect the batteries from French raids although the workers had to endure occasional fire from isolated snipers.

At 1900 hrs on the twelfth the British batteries were ready. The guns and mortars rapidly found the range and, gradually, the lower town was virtually levelled by the relentless bombardment.

26/6/1759	3/7	10/7	14/7	21/7	28/7	4/8	11/8	18/8	25/8	1/9	8/9	12/9	13/9(0400hrs)	(0700hrs)	(0830hrs)	(1000hrs)	(1130hrs)
pages 65-67			70-74		75-77			78-80			81-83			84-91			92-95

PRELIMINARIES

31st July 1759

The Battle of Montmorency

According to a plan mentioned by Wolfe to Monckton on 28 July, four companies of grenadiers were to land and take a small French battery – the Johnstone battery – on the beach, below the cliff of the Beauport shore, not very far west of the falls at Montmorency. A vessel was to run aground with the four grenadier companies; the grenadiers from the other regiments would be in other vessels in reserve. This minor operation was to take place on the 30th.

However, as the hours passed, Wolfe began to wonder if it might not be the opportunity for something much grander: to break the French defences and establish a British 'beach head' on the Beauport shore. If that could be done, the French troops on the west shore of the Montmorency River would be compelled to give up their position and the British troops on the east shore could cross and join the grenadiers. Before long, most of the army could be there – thousands of regular troops – and move towards Québec. So, in order to prevent this, Wolfe's reasoning went, Montcalm would have to come down to the shore with his troops and attack the British on the beach. In an unfavourable position with fewer regulars, Montcalm would most likely be beaten.

Wolfe must have taken the decision to modify the raid into a full-scale landing all by himself, with no consultations with his brigadiers and senior naval officers. He apparently did not mention this new vision of things to come until the next day in a note to Brigadier Monckton. Presumably Saunders would have learned of the change, which called for additional naval resources, at that time also. In the event, on the 30th, there was a flat calm with no wind at all, not even a slight breeze. The ships could not move and the attack had to be cancelled. By that time, the two other brigadiers had learned about Wolfe's new plan. It seems that all three had serious reservations about it. What if Montcalm

Montcalm's headquarters, formerly the house of Monsieur de Vienne, in the centre of the Beauport Lines. (National Archive of Canada, C1089)

would not come down with his battalions to eliminate the British beach head? What if the French remained well entrenched on top of the hill and repulsed British assaults? It would be very difficult getting up the steep cliff under fire. And those who did make it then still had to overcome strong French positions at the top, by then likely filled with regular soldiers with more reinforcements arriving all the time to support them.

The brigadiers' opinions may seem, at first glance even today, to be too pessimistic. But they must have had in mind that Montcalm, for what they knew of him, might not come out but instead fight from a covered position. This is what he had done at Ticonderoga the previous year in a less favourable position than the Beauport shore cliffs. The Anglo-Americans had withdrawn after suffering terrible losses in the failed assaults. Obviously, the brigadiers were apprehensive of another costly repulse. Another worry was that the Royal Navy's ships would not be able to bombard the beach redoubts effectively. Wolfe listened to their arguments and their dislike of his much expanded plan. But Wolfe was a man

26/6/1759	3/7	10/7	14/7	21/7	28/7	4/8	11/8	18/8	25/8	1/9	8/9	12/9	13/9(0400hrs)	(0700hrs)	(0830hrs)	(1000hrs)	(1130hrs)
pages 65-67 & 68-69				75-77			78-80			81-83			84-91				92-95

of action and as 'nothing better (was) proposed' by his senior officers, he decided to go ahead.

If it had its tactical flaws, Wolfe's new plan for taking Montmorency and the Beauport shore was certainly good for the morale of his soldiers. Over a month had passed without a real chance to get at the French. Perhaps, if left to sit and wait for too long, they might become less keen. At this point in time, the men were full of hope and did not doubt that a brave and determined assault would carry the French positions. On the morning of the 31st, the sun rose to a very clear and sunny day. It was very warm. Most of all there was a breeze so the ships could move. The British attack was on. The troops were on the transports which now slowly moved closer to shore, west of the Montmorency Falls. The assault was to be led by the grenadier companies of all the regiments, specifically the grenadiers from the 15th, 28th, 35th, 43rd, 47th, 40th, 58th, 2/60th, 3/60th, 78th and the three companies of Louisbourg Grenadiers for a total of 13 companies. It was the cream of the army, around 1,000 of Wolfe's best fighting men. Another 200 men from the 60th and part of the 15th and 78th were in reserve under Monckton. Townshend's and Murray's forces were to join them by marching across the ford from the British

camp on the east side of the Montmorency River and attack the more easterly Sault battery. A feint would be made by the light infantry, the rangers and Anstruther's 58th Foot by marching up the Montmorency River as if they would try to ford it upstream. Thus, almost overnight, a minor operation had become a major attempt to break the French lines.

The element of surprise was apparently not considered vital nor was it achieved. During the night of 30–31 July, Lieutenant Jean-Baptiste d'Alleyrac of the Languedoc Regiment was in a bivouac on the Beauport shore when he perceived much movement in the British ships. He warned his superiors and by early morning, the French were on full alert with more troops moving into the positions on the cliff. By 1100 hrs, two British 20-gun vessels with the leading grenadier companies had run aground as planned in front of their objective, the Johnstone battery. A few minutes later the 60-gun

The plan was for the grenadiers to be landed by boat to scale the cliffs. They would be reinforced by troops, crossing the mouth of the Montmorency River, which was fordable at low tide, and attacking along the beach. Meanwhile a feint attack would be made up the Montmorency River towards the ford.

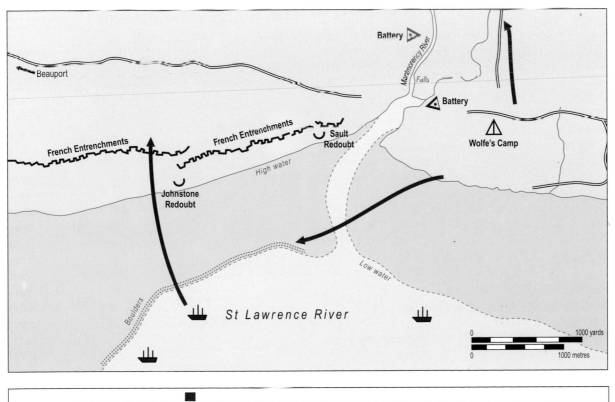

26/6/1759	3/7	10/7	14/7	21/7	28/7	4/8	11/8	18/8	25/8	1/9	8/9	12/9	13/9(0400hrs)	(0700hrs)	(0830hrs)	(1000hrs)	(1130hrs)
pages 65-67 & 68-69					75-77		78-80		81-83			84-91			92-95		

Wolfe's attack on the Beauport Lines with the Montmorency Falls on the right, 31 July 1759.
(Print after Hervey Smith. National Archives of Canada, C782)

HMS *Centurion* approached the Sault battery. The British ships opened fire on the batteries. It was over an hour before the rest of the grenadiers, the 15th and the 78th arrived off the beach in about 200 longboats. There were difficulties for the boats as they encountered a line of boulder reefs about 500 yards from the shore. All the soldiers then sat in the boats waiting for the signal to land and attack while a way around the boulders was found. A messenger was sent to Townshend telling him to move his troops no further towards the Sault battery. The few French cannons in the batteries opened up but caused no damage. With much delay already, the operation was not off to a good start. Admiral Saunders now provided Wolfe with a flat-bottomed boat and a naval officer to find a way around the boulder reefs and select a spot to land the troops.

All these movements were carefully watched by the French. That most eastern sector (or left flank) of the French defences was under the direct command of the cool-headed General Lévis. Montcalm was actually much further west at his HQ at the village of Beauport. Meanwhile, at the Montmorency River which was at the very end of the French eastern sector, Captain De Repentigny's colonial troop scouts had spotted numerous British troops moving up their side of the river and were shadowing them. General Lévis was warned at about 1300 hrs and thought it was a feint but sent

Captain Duprat of the colonial troops with 500 men and Indians as reinforcements to the area, just in case. They were to follow the British movement. The Royal-Roussillon Regiment, further west but the closest to the area, was ordered to move up.

At the same time, Lévis could also see much boat movement in the St Lawrence coming from Point Levy and the Ile d'Orléans. Feeling the position just west of the Montmorency Falls to be too weakly manned, he ordered the two Montréal militia battalions posted in the area to be on full alert and to be in constant communication with Royal-Roussillon. Thus, Lévis was ready on all sides. At about 1330 hrs, Anstruther's 58th was reported moving towards a ford on the upper Montmorency River. The 500 militiamen and Indians were in the area on the west side of the shore, watching from the woods to see what the British would actually do. By now, the Royal-Roussillon Regiment was posted between the militia and Indians, and the Béarn Regiment, which was stationed near the Montmorency Falls. At 1400 hrs, Montcalm arrived to join Lévis, telling him that the Guyenne Regiment would be up shortly with two additional companies of grenadiers (one was from La Sarre) and 100 Trois-Rivières militiamen as reinforcements and reserves. Montcalm and Lévis agreed that if the west side was attacked, its troops would be reinforced by the units in reserve posted at the centre of the sector.

Observing the various British boat movements, Lévis sensed that the landing would likely come on the beach west of the falls, between or on the Sault and Johnstone

26/6/1759	3/7	10/7	14/7	21/7	28/7	4/8	11/8	18/8	25/8	1/9	8/9	12/9	13/9(0400hrs)	(0700hrs)	(0830hrs)	(1000hrs)	(1130hrs)
pages 65-67 & 68-69				75-77			78-80			81-83			84-91				92-95

redoubts. He accordingly ordered a battalion of the Montréal militia positioned as skirmishers on the beach between the two redoubts, the other Montréal militia battalion up the cliff with the La Sarre grenadiers. By early afternoon, many boats full of troops could be observed from the top of the cliff. Bombardment of the beach redoubts from the British ships was very heavy. Lévis felt that the men in the Johnstone redoubt and on that part of the beach would not stand much chance of stopping a major assault on the beach and eventually ordered their evacuation to positions up on the cliff.

In the middle of the afternoon, Lévis received notice from Captain Duprat that Anstruther's 58th Foot was withdrawing from the ford on the upper Montmorency River and was retiring. Wolfe's feint had totally failed and Lévis was now sure there would be no attack from there. He immediately sent his ADC, the Scottish Jacobite Chevalier de Johnstone, with orders to bring back to the shore area Captain Duprat's Canadian militia, Indians and the Royal-Roussillon Regiment.

Meanwhile, Wolfe was on the flat-bottomed boat looking for a suitable passage and landing place. He could see much activity by the French at the crest of the

The grenadiers failed to scale the cliffs and were repulsed. The attack was called off and both Townshend's and Murray's troops, together with the remaining grenadiers, retreated back along the beach to escape the rising tide.

cliffs. For some reason, he interpreted the French troops' hustle and bustle, wrongly, to be 'confusion and disorder' and this convinced him that the attack should be made. The landing spot finally selected was dead on the Johnstone redoubt, and just to the west of it. The boats full of grenadiers finally moved and formed up, passing between the shoals and rowed towards the beach. By then, it was late in the afternoon, about 1700 hrs, and much time had been wasted. The clear, sunny and very warm weather of a typical July day in Canada was quickly becoming overcast, with dark and low clouds moving in over the area.

At last the boats beached and the 13 companies of grenadiers jumped out, waist deep in the water according to a grenadier officer, and charged up the beach, full of warlike spirit, confident of carrying just about anything at bayonet point. Within minutes, they were all over the beach but found the redoubt empty and the French gone, seemingly on the run in terror of their bayonets. As per Wolfe's orders, the drummers now beat the 'Grenadier's March' which 'animated our Men so much that we (officers) could scarce restrain them.' The grenadiers' high spirits were now at a peak and despite their usual good discipline, impetuosity got the better of them and they began scaling the cliff to get at the French. Whether this was done because the officers lost control of their over-enthusiastic grenadiers or whether some of the officers themselves were in the same wild spirits, the result was a badly-timed move up

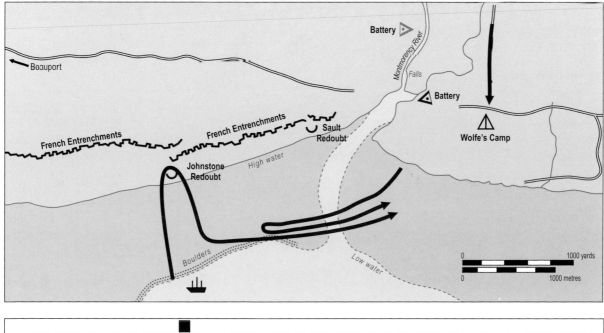

26/6/1759	3/7	10/7	14/7	21/7	28/7	4/8	11/8	18/8	25/8	1/9	8/9	12/9	13/9(0400hrs)	(0700hrs)	(0830hrs)	(1000hrs)	(1130hrs)
pages 65-67 & 68-69				75-77		78-80			81-83				84-91			92-95	

the hill. And it was contrary to Wolfe's orders which called on the grenadier companies to form on the beach, once the redoubt was taken and French skirmishers cleared, and wait for Monckton's 15th Foot and 78th Foot 'second wave' to land, and for Townshend's and Murray's men to make it across the ford below the Montmorency Falls.

What Lévis saw instead was a 'column' of redcoats on the beach which started to climb the cliff. He already had moved up the Royal-Roussillon and Guyenne battalions to counter this attack. The Canadian militiamen and French soldiers, well entrenched on top of the cliff, opened up a brisk fire on them as they came up, taking a heavy toll within minutes. With Wolfe's plan in ruins, the purplish black clouds overhead suddenly burst in thunder, lightning and torrential rain – 'the dreadfullest thunder-storm and fall of rain that can be conceived' related Knox. 'A furious thunder-storm veiled them and hid their movements from us' noted Lévis. It was one of those sudden thunder-storms, familiar to Canadians, and provoked by the very hot and humid Canadian summers. Gunfire stopped as everyone's powder became wet in the massive downpour. It should have been a good chance for the British grenadiers to reach the top unhindered by musketry. But the rain had made the grass of the steep slopes very slippery, visibility was almost nil and, by now, most of the grenadiers' formations were totally disorganised. The attack ground to a halt.

Wolfe, by now on the beach with some of Amherst's 15th and Fraser's 78th knew the attack had failed and he feared that the retreat of Townshend's and Murray's brigades across the ford further east could be cut off. According to Lévis' and Montcalm's journals, the French had no such plans but much time had passed and another dangerous and formidable foe was advancing – the tide was rising.

The order to retire was given. As the rain cleared and the storm subsided, the French and Canadians could see the British again. They had gone down to the beach and, according to Lévis, 'we could see them behind their vessels and were filling their boats with their wounded and with all the troops they could contain.' The rest of the British troops retired along the beach past the Sault redoubt. These included part of Fraser's 78th which was covering the retreat of the surviving hapless grenadiers. They met Townshend and his troops coming up. They had already passed the falls and now were told to retire. Wolfe and the brigadiers

The Indians move in following the repulse of the British grenadiers' attack at Montmorency. (Print after J. Macfarlane)

marched with them going back to the British camp on the east side of the Montmorency.

Meanwhile, the Indians allied to the French now quickly moved in to finish off and scalp the wounded and dead, take prisoners that they would sell or keep and pick up trophies, as was their custom. This was a practice condemned by both the French and the British but the Indians wanted their prizes and made sure to be on the spot after a battle. French and Canadian troops soon arrived to rescue the remaining wounded and buy off the others.

Meanwhile, the Highlanders of Fraser's 78th with Wolfe stopped at the ford farther east and two companies refused to retire further until all the wounded who could be carried off were safe from the Indians and French. Having rescued as many as possible, the stubborn Highlanders consented to cross the ford. It was high time as 'ye tide of flood was so high that the Regiments could scarcely wade over ye ford' recalled Townshend.

The assault on the Beauport lines had proved an abject failure. The French had few casualties, Lévis reporting losses of about twenty to thirty officers and men, mostly wounded. For the British, it was many times worse. Wolfe reported losing 210 killed and 230 wounded. And they were among the best and bravest men in his army. Grenadier poet Ned Botwood was among the unfortunates and was given so much 'hot stuff' by the French and Canadians that it killed him.

26/6/1759	3/7	10/7	14/7	21/7	28/7	4/8	11/8	18/8	25/8	1/9	8/9	12/9	13/9(0400hrs)	(0700hrs)	(0830hrs)	(1000hrs)	(1130hrs)
pages 65-67 & 68-69				75-77			78-80			81-83			84-91				92-95

PRELIMINARIES

July – August 1759

Raids and Fighting Patrols

The first large engagement during the siege had thus been a victory for Montcalm. It was the second time in little more than a year that the French troops had beaten off a determined assault by a powerful enemy. Their triumph at Ticonderoga occurred in July of 1758. In all, the French with Lévis were perhaps two thousand; about half French metropolitan troops with a few colonial troops, the rest being militiamen in large numbers. The Indians had played no significant part in the British debacle. So confidence – which at times had been sagging – was high In the French camp. They just might, they thought, be able to resist until the fall when the British would have to leave.

In the British camp, all was gloom. One of every four grenadiers had been hit in the brief assault on the unscalable cliff. Of these, some were nursing their wounds at the hospital or in camp while one in eight would be seen no more by his comrades. But the men, elite soldiers all, were not discouraged and craved for revenge. If only their generals could give them a decent chance to get at the French.

In the generals' quarters, the mood was even more sombre. The attempt had failed miserably as the brigadiers had predicted. True, they had no plan up their sleeve then but now they also had to deal with a serious blow which might affect morale. And time was ticking away. The siege was now into August. The pressure on Wolfe was mounting. It seems there were bitter words especially from Townshend and, surprisingly, from Colonel Carleton. In any event, as the commander, Wolfe had to find a solution, offer a new plan but he could not come up with anything viable. Neither could his brigadiers. It was not for lack of talent of these men, all excellent officers. But the natural might of Québec, ably defended as it had been up to now, was enough to cause the most brilliant tactician to throw up his hands in despair. Particularly after Montmorency, there seemed

to be no way to crack the defences. The spectre of failure now reared its head, a distant prospect yet, but real enough for generals who could anticipate shame and broken careers if a solution could not be found.

To keep spirits up, Wolfe decided to use the river which was controlled by the Royal Navy's ships for raids up and down the coast. It would keep the French on their toes and cause considerable damage while keeping the British forces busy. On 3 August, Brigadier Murray was ordered up the St Lawrence River, past Québec, to raid whatever could be destroyed up to Trois-Rivières. The French forces could not counter such moves on the river and would have to divert forces to follow the ships. Bougainville was put in charge of such a corps, numbering a thousand men including most of the cavalry, to follow British ship movements up river. On 8 August, Murray attempted to land at Pointe-aux-Trembles but Bougainville lay waiting and the British soldiers and sailors were beaten back with losses of some 140 killed and wounded. Murray lurked for ten days and then made a successful raid on the village of Deschambault, finding no opposition. Some of the spare equipment of the French metropolitan troops was stored in a house there and it was burned. Some sporadic and ineffective firing on the redcoats was noted, probably by isolated local militiamen, but when Bougainville's cavalry and Indians eventually came up, Murray's men simply re-embarked.

These raids worried Montcalm, not so much for the potential material damage, but for fear that his line of

A typical Canadian farmhouse of the 18th century. Wolfe's policy of putting many such places to the torch achieved no military objective.

26/6/1759	3/7	10/7	14/7	21/7	28/7	4/8	11/8	18/8	25/8	1/9	8/9	12/9	13/9(0400hrs)	(0700hrs)	(0830hrs)	(1000hrs)	(1130hrs)
pages 65-67 & 68-69			70-74				78-80			81-83			84-91			92-95	

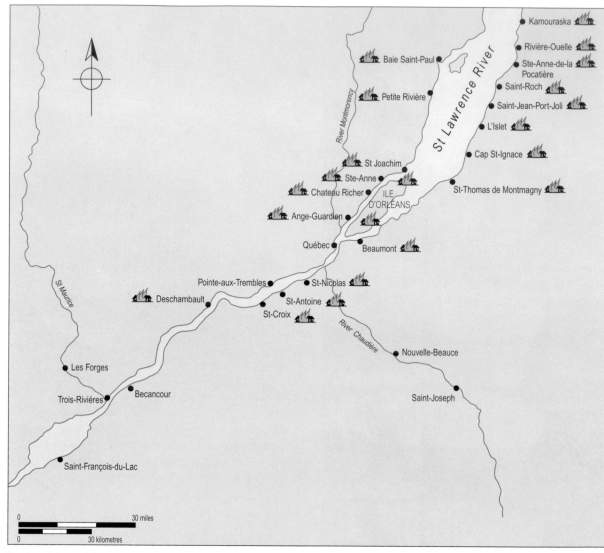

During July and August 1759, General Wolfe launched a series of raids and fighting patrols up and down the St Lawrence from Québec. The attacks up-river towards Trois-Rivières particularly worried Montcalm, who feared his lines of communication with Montréal might be cut.

communications with Trois-Rivières and Montréal might be severed. He feared the British might choose a strong position and entrench themselves. Hearing of the raid on Deschambault, Montcalm hurried to Bougainville's assistance with a party of grenadiers but turned back on the way when he learned that the British had gone back to their vessels. Montcalm's move seemed very hasty and ill-advised to Vaudreuil who obviously, and probably

rightly, felt that the position could be easily turned and communications would not be cut. Murray finally returned to Point Levy on 25 August having accomplished little.

Simultaneously, Wolfe had issued orders to Monckton which amounted to nothing less than laying the country to waste. Monckton cringed at such orders and sought confirmation. It was confirmed and so parties of American rangers with detachments of British troops went out to do the grim duty. On 4 August, they destroyed the settlement at Baie Saint-Paul. By 6 August, the destructive work had been extended to burning 'all the houses from the village of St Joachim to the Montmorency River' on the north shore and from the Chaudière River down to Beaumont near

26/6/1759	3/7	10/7	14/7	21/7	28/7	4/8	11/8	18/8	25/8	1/9	8/9	12/9	13/9(0400hrs)	(0700hrs)	(0830hrs)	(1000hrs)	(1130hrs)
pages 65-67 & 68-69			70-74				78-80				81-83		84-91				92-95

Monckton's camp. Every 'house and hutt' was to be burned down except for the village churches. This, Wolfe wrote, was supposed to lure Montcalm out of his entrenched positions and allow the British to beat him in a general engagement.

It did not make much sense as most of the destruction would be on the south shore. How could the French army cross over there anyway? And Montcalm was not likely to try storming the British fortified camp at Montmorency. Even if he took it, he could then easily be cut off as he moved east to chase the firebrands. The rangers were probably the best choice of troops for this sort of duty as they had in mind tales of destruction in New England by parties of French and Indians. Here was a chance for retribution but deep down, many of them must have felt it was a coward's war against civilians. There was certainly no glory in it. The civilians in the unfortunate villages were caught in a dilemma. On the one hand, they were all militiamen and, by law and

The church of Sainte-Anne-de-Beaupré. As in many villages east of Québec laid to waste on Wolfe's orders, the church was the only building left standing.

patriotic duty, bound to resist the enemy. On the other, although they had been fairly quiet since the British had appeared, apart from the occasional pot shots, it seemed nothing would satisfy the darker side of Wolfe's personality which not content with mere neutrality sought to reduce them to outright destitution. Throughout August, scenes of desolation worthy of modern conflicts in the Balkans were commonplace. Village after village went up in smoke after being looted and the livestock slaughtered if not seized. By

September, it was estimated that about 1,400 farmers' houses had been destroyed by fire besides barns and huts. This created thousands of refugees who fled to Québec with tales of terror while others sought refuge in the forest. Doubtless many of the young and the elderly, unable to withstand the exposure, perished although no figure will ever be known.

When there was resistance, it was most savagely dealt with. On 23 August for instance, Captain Montgomery of the 43rd with about 300 men encountered resistance from Canadian militiamen at Sainte-Anne (today the shrine town of Sainte-Anne-de-Beaupré). Five British soldiers were wounded but the thirty or so Canadians were 'surrounded, killed and scalped' having – according to Knox – disguised themselves as Indians. Ensign Malcolm Fraser of the 78th was there and consigned in his private journal that 'the barbarous Captain Montgomery, who commanded us all, ordered (the prisoners) to be butchered in a most inhuman and cruel manner...' Senior officers too were appalled at what Wolfe's orders had brought. Townshend, especially disgusted, confided to his wife, Lady Ferrers, also a peer, that he had 'never served so disagreeable a Campaign as this, Our unequal Force has reduced our Operation to a Scene of Skirmish, Cruelty & Devastation. It is War of the worst Shape...'

All this did not impress Montcalm very much. It was all part of war in America which was seen as more barbarous than in Europe. With some scorn for the British troops perpetrating such deeds, he mentioned in his journal on 23 August that 'those people apparently do not wish to attempt any sort of landing unless they find absolutely no resistance. They continue to burn below the Montmorency, on Ile d'Orléans and the south shore.' Thus, at the end of August, Wolfe had laid the countryside to waste but failed again in his stated objective: to goad Montcalm out. On the contrary, Montcalm was even starting to wonder if the British might not have to think of their own departure. But in his journal on 27 August, he made a prophetic entry: '...it would be singular if M. Wolfe kept (his actions to setting) fires, ravages (and) a single, rather badly conducted attempt (to land) which cost him four hundred grenadiers, on 31 July, and bore no fruit; he requires a bold stroke, a thunderbolt.'

26/6/1759	3/7	10/7	14/7	21/7	28/7	4/8	11/8	18/8	25/8	1/9	8/9	12/9	13/9(0400hrs)	(0700hrs)	(0830hrs)	(1000hrs)	(1130hrs)
pages 65-67 & 68-69			70-74				78-80		81-83			84-91				92-95	

THE HEIGHTS OF ABRAHAM

Preparations

On 29 August, Townshend, Murray and Monckton met and drafted an important proposal to Wolfe. First, they stated that any attack on the Beauport shore was doomed as had been the attempt at Montmorency on 31 July. A month later, the French engineers would have made the redoubts even stronger and the troops there were as vigilant and as numerous as ever. Indeed, no more attacks in that area should be made, and the camp at Montmorency should be abandoned and the troops moved to the south shore to join the other part of the army. This would end the deadlock and create a strong body of troops to attempt to break the French defences elsewhere. The area where the brigadiers felt this should be done was 'above the Town' past Cape Diamond.

As a result, a conference with the three brigadiers and Admiral Saunders was held by an intrigued Wolfe on the morning of 31 August. By then, Admiral Saunders and his officers had been briefed by the brigadiers and supported the plan. Wolfe agreed as well and that afternoon, the British at Montmorency started moving out their supplies and guns to Point Levy although it was not until 1 September that the troops were given the order to evacuate.

Wolfe seems to have had some misgivings about this. In a letter to Admiral Saunders, he mentioned that his sickly condition had prevented him from executing his 'own plan'. This has been interpreted in various ways by historians but the latest consensus is that Wolfe's 'own plan' simply meant his very recent proposals to again attack the Beauport shore. He still had hopes about goading Montcalm to attack him in that area. On 3 September, various movements by the troops and fleet were made in the hope that the French would believe that only a weak battalion was left at Montmorency. It was further hoped by Wolfe that Montcalm would come out with his troops to catch it.

He would then be caught by five battalions nearby. But Montcalm feared a trap, did nothing and all the British troops were finally evacuated out of Montmorency by 4 September. Shortly thereafter, the militiamen of Ange-Gardien, the village near the site of the abandoned British camp, came to see what was left. They found their homes destroyed, the fruit trees cut down in what had once been gardens, but the crops in the fields had been left to grow.

To Montcalm, the abandonment of Montmorency by the British and the many ship and boat movements up and down the river were most likely feints. He felt that Wolfe had not really given up on a landing on the Beauport shore although it might now occur further to the west, possibly at La Canardière or even at the St Charles River. So he repositioned some of his troops. Royal-Roussillon and Repentigny's militiamen and colonial soldiers were moved to the area of the village of Beauport. Guyenne was put on the right, near the St Charles River, in a position where it could quickly march to the west side of the city if need be, as Montcalm noted. These were minor moves and the French forces remained deployed essentially in the same area. For his part, Vaudreuil had more concerns about a British landing above the town at Anse-des-Mères, near Anse-au-Foulon, and transmitted his concern to Montcalm who naturally greeted this opinion with his usual sarcasm, as with anything that came from the governor-general. Montcalm was sure that 100 alert men could stop any landing in that area long enough for his battalions to come over. Probably true enough if the men were alert... However, he did instruct Bougainville to keep his observation corps ahead of the British ships moving up the river. This unfortunate instruction put Bougainville's Corps even farther away from the city. Montcalm had thus totally misread the latest British manoeuvres.

26/6/1759	3/7	10/7	14/7	21/7	28/7	4/8	11/8	18/8	25/8	1/9	8/9	12/9	13/9(0400hrs)	(0700hrs)	(0830hrs)	(1000hrs)	(1130hrs)
pages 65-67 & 68-69			70-74		75-77						81-83			84-91			92-95	

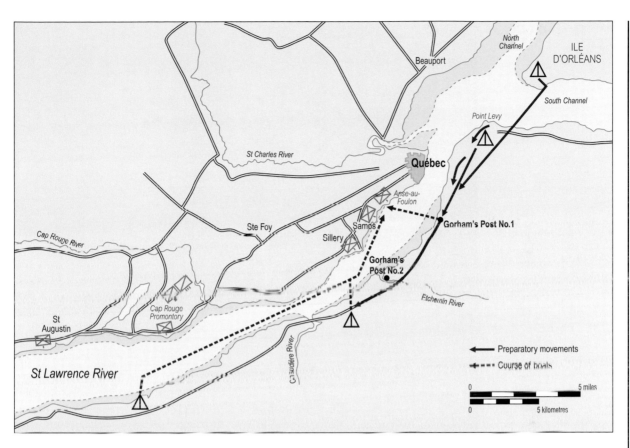

Wolfe deployed his troops at various points along the south shore of the river so as not to give away his intended landing place to Bougainville's pickets on the opposite bank. When the initial landings came at Anse-au-Foulon, reinforcements were moved rapidly across the St Lawrence from Gorham's Post No.1.

At this time, Bougainville's Corps had some of the elite of Montcalm's army. It consisted of the five grenadier companies of the metropolitan regiments with detachments from the regiments acting as light infantry, picked Canadian volunteers who served as light infantry, the 200 troopers of the Corps of Cavalry totalling about 1,500 men plus several hundred Indians.

For the British, the next thing to do was to find a suitable place for an attack above the town. During the first week of September, a good part of the brigadiers' plan was carried out. A force of up to 3,600 men was gathered on the ships and readied for the future attempt. On 7 September, the British squadron was up river near Cap Rouge, watched from the north shore by Bougainville's troops. As the French cavalry troopers watched from a distance, Wolfe and his officers had another meeting to reorganise the three brigades out of the available troops. The 1st brigade was under Brigadier-General Monckton and was made up of Amherst's 15th, Kennedy's 43rd and Lawrence's 3/60th. The 2nd was under Brigadier-General Townshend and had Bragg's 28th, Lascelles' 47th and Fraser's 78th. The 3rd, led by Brigadier-General Murray, comprised Otway's 35th, Anstruther's 58th and the Louisbourg Grenadiers. Later that day, Wolfe and the brigadiers went up river to Pointe-aux-Trembles looking for a likely spot. On 8 and 9 September, it rained heavily which prevented a landing which would have occurred 'a little below' Pointe-aux-Trembles according to Chief Engineer Mackellar.

Undaunted if not particularly optimistic, Wolfe made reconnaissance on his own, searching for another spot to land his troops. The Pointe-aux-Trembles area was now passed over. This time, the brigadiers would not be part of the decision for the new landing site. It would be solely Wolfe's decision and by 10 September, he had chosen Anse-au-Foulon.

26/6/1759	3/7	10/7	14/7	21/7	28/7	4/8	11/8	18/8	25/8	1/9	8/9	12/9	13/9(0400hrs)	(0700hrs)	(0830hrs)	(1000hrs)	(1130hrs)
pages 65-67 & 68-69			70-74		75-77					81-83			84-91			92-95	

The cove at Anse-au-Foulon, with the Plains of Abraham stretching away to Québec city on the left. Why Wolfe chose this site for his landings is uncertain.
(Print after Hervey Smyth. National Archives of Canada, C788)

Why Anse-au-Foulon in particular remains something of a mystery. A fantastic and entirely unfounded reason was postulated in 1921 by Major-General R.H. Mahon in his biography of James Murray. It will be recalled that Bougainville commanded the French observation corps west of the city. In order for the British landing to succeed according to Mahon, on the fatal night of the landing Bougainville was lured away from his post for the evening by a certain Madame de Vienne 'a lady of notoriety and charm'. She was acting, the tale goes on, in the interest of Intendant Bigot and Cadet who feared a French victory as it would expose their crooked financial dealings. Once they knew that Bougainville had been lured away, they sent word by a deserter to Wolfe that the landing at Anse-au-Foulon could safely proceed!

No sources were given for this by Mahon although one suspects William Kirby's 'The Golden Dog', a 19th century novel set in the last days of the French Régime, as the inspiration. Madame de Vienne was actually a housewife who lived with her mother and her husband. And she was indeed very well known to Bougainville. He had been quartered at the Vienne's house at Beauport since 1756 as she was the wife of his cousin François-Joseph de Vienne, the interim storekeeper at Québec. François-Joseph de Vienne was not, incidentally, one of the 'insiders' of Intendant Bigot's gang. By his own account, Bougainville was at Cap Rouge that night. There is no evidence of any contacts between Wolfe,

Bigot and Cadet and while the Intendant and his associate were certainly lining their pockets, they were not traitors. In the event, they were brought to trial anyway after the French defeat, Bigot being banished from France for life. Finally, why should Wolfe have trusted Bigot and Cadet?

Whatever the reason Wolfe came to choose Anse-au-Foulon, he did not inform his brigadiers about it and made preparations on his own. Navy officers were warned of an impending operation and got their landing craft ready. Another thousand men were detached to the ships from Point Levy and Ile d'Orléans. He did, however, inform his friend Lieutenant-Colonel Burton of the 48th on 10 September about trying something at Foulon. Thus, the 'security' which was later invoked as Wolfe's reason for not involving his brigadiers makes little sense. Some animosity toward the brigadiers might be a more valid reason. In any event, an operation was being prepared and on 12 September, the three brigadiers co-signed a respectful letter to Wolfe stating they were 'not sufficiently informed ... particularly to the place or places we are to attack'. Wolfe's answer, made to Monckton, was far more curt and pointed out that the 'place is called Foulon', that it was 'not the usual thing to point out in publick orders the direct spot of an attack', nor 'for any inferior Officer not charged with a particular duty to ask instructions upon that point (the attack)'. He added that it was his own duty to attack the French and that he would answer 'to his Majesty & the Publick for the consequences.' Bluntly put, he alone would decide and expected his officers to obey his orders without question or comments when they received them.

26/6/1759	3/7	10/7	14/7	21/7	28/7	4/8	11/8	18/8	25/8	1/9	8/9	12/9	13/9(0400hrs)	(0700hrs)	(0830hrs)	(1000hrs)	(1130hrs)
pages 65-67 & 68-69			70-74		75-77							81-83			84-91		92-95

THE HEIGHTS OF ABRAHAM

12th/13th September 1759

Amphibious Assault

ate in the evening of 12 September, thousands of British soldiers were standing quietly on the decks of the ships and waiting to get into the many barges and longboats. Some 30 flat bottomed landing barges were to carry the majority of the troops. At the head were eight barges that would carry Colonel Howe's light infantry, followed by six barges with Bragg's 28th, four barges with Kennedy's 43rd, five barges with Lascelle's 47th and six barges bearing Anstruther's 58th. Following this first wave was another barge with a large number of longboats with part of Fraser's 78th, Amherst's 15th, Otway's 35th, the Louisbourg Grenadiers, part of the 2nd and 3rd battalions of the 60th Royal American and three field guns with Royal Artillery gunners. In reserve would be Webb's 48th. Each soldier was given a ration of rum to mix with water in his canteen and two days food rations besides his weapons and ammunition. Blankets, tents and other supplies would be sent on later.

All now knew the landing was on and that the next day would be the decisive one. Naturally, a feint had been prepared. At about 2300 hrs, boats filled with marines from the main part of the fleet that had assembled off Point Levy now heaved away and headed towards the Beauport shore in the dark. From there, they rowed back and forth between the St Charles River and the village of Beauport at a distance from the shore, keeping this up until 0400 hrs on 13 September. Some of the ships had also come closer to the shore at La Canardière and fired off occasional broadsides at it for most of the night. The batteries at Point Levy also opened up on the city during the night. After a while, Montcalm concluded nothing much was going to happen at Beauport. His soldiers were tired and he sent them to rest.

Meanwhile the British troops were boarding the barges and longboats in the late evening of 12

Model of the type of landing barge used to transport British troops to Anse-au-Foulon.
(National Maritime Museum, London)

September. Early on the 13th, at about 0200 hrs, they heaved off and started silently towards Anse-au-Foulon. The weather was fine, the night calm. The moon had been up since about 2200 hrs but it was in its last quarter and gave little light. In the first boat was a 24-man detachment of Howe's light infantry, all volunteers, who would be the first on shore to secure the foot of the cliff. Wolfe is said to have been in one of the first boats not far behind. He had issued orders for the strictest silence to be obeyed by all. Thus, the rather romantic legend about his reciting poetry from Gray's *Elegy in a Country Churchyard* (finishing with the lines: 'Awaits alike th' inevitable hour. The paths of glory lead but to the grave') as his boat approached the enemy shore makes no sense at all. It was hardly the example and the spirit Wolfe would have wanted to set for his army!

Some 175 feet above the river on top of the cliff French sentinels watched for movements in the night. The area was guarded by a party of militiamen from Lorette under the command of colonial troops Captain

26/6/1759	3/7	10/7	14/7 21/7	28/7 4/8	11/8 18/8	25/8	1/9	8/9 12/9	13/9(0400hrs)	(0700hrs)	(0830hrs)	(1000hrs)	(1130hrs)
pages 65-67 & 68-69			70-74	75-77	78-80					84-91		92-95	

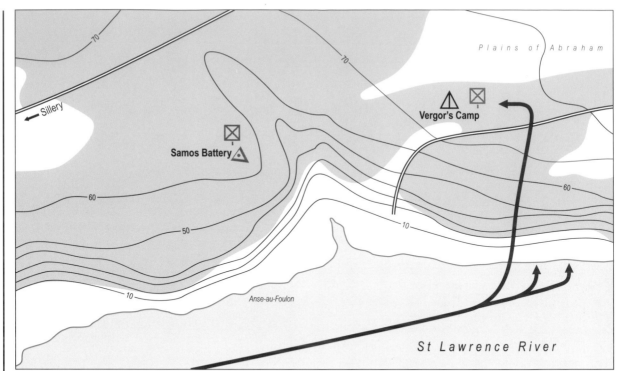

The Anse-au-Foulon and the edge of the Plains of Abraham with French picket positions. The arrows indicate the approximate positions of the British forces which landed and scaled the heights in the dark.

Vergor. By a very lucky coincidence for the British, a French boat convoy of grain and supplies was expected during the night and the sentries at Anse-au-Foulon had been warned to expect it. Its passage was later cancelled but word of this had not reached the sentries when the British boats appeared.

As they came closer to Anse-au-Foulon, a challenge was heard from a French sentry, 'Qui vive?' In one of the lead boats was Captain Fraser of the 78th Highlanders who, Townshend later wrote, 'had been in ye Dutch Service & spoke french'. There are several versions of what happened next. Townshend mentions that Fraser answered 'la france & vive le Roy (France and Long Live the King), on which ye French Centinels ran along ye Shore in ye dark crying laissez passer ils sont nos Gens avec les provisions (Let them pass, they are our people with the supplies)'. Intendant Bigot also reported that 'France' was the reply to the challenge and the boats were allowed to pass. Still another version has it that after Fraser had answered 'France', the sentry asked 'why don't you speak louder?' to which the wily Scot told the sentry to keep his voice down as the British might hear them.

The best known version, of unknown origin, has been repeated for well over a century and says that Captain

Fraser's answer was 'La Reine' indicating one of the French metropolitan regiments. The problem is that La Reine was not part of the Québec garrison but was posted on Lake Champlain and so would have immediately raised suspicion.

Captain Vergor who was in charge of the post also left an account, still almost unknown, of the event. He had been warned of the supply boats coming and at 0300 hrs his men spotted them. He came to the area and had the sentry ask 'who were the boats, from what regiment, and where were they headed...to which they answered France, Marine and that they were carrying supplies to Québec.' Thus, the first answer was 'France' for the identity of the convoy. The second reply 'Marine' for regiment could mean Navy or indicate the colonial Compagnies franches de la Marine. The words 'La Reine' and 'Marine' have something of the same sound. The boats passed on.

The first British troops arrived at Anse-au-Foulon, still undetected. As they landed, Howe's light infantrymen

26/6/1759	3/7	10/7	14/7	21/7	28/7	4/8	11/8	18/8	25/8	1/9	8/9	12/9	13/9(0400hrs)	(0700hrs)	(0830hrs)	(1000hrs)	(1130hrs)
pages 65-67 & 68-69			70-74		75-77			78-80								84-91	92-95

British troops landing at the Anse-au-Foulon before scaling the Heights of Abraham.
(National Army Museum, London)

found themselves in the dark at the foot of a very steep cliff. One can visualise a bold Colonel Howe whispering to Major Delauney that a way up must be found at once even if it meant going straight up. The surface of the cliff is brittle rock interspaced with small trees and stumps. Nevertheless, some of the soldiers – but probably only a few companies – went straight up and climbed with difficulty, pulling themselves up by the small trees. Delauney, a 'very active & enterprising Officer' according to Townshend, had found a possible way up 'higher up ye River' by means of a narrow path. This path, called a 'narrow precipice with an abbatis & a battery above it' by Townshend, was most likely situated a bit further to the west, about 400 metres from the landing place below. The precipice was a bit lower and the slope not as steep. It was still dark and the French had not yet given the alarm.

The vanguard of light infantrymen managed to get up the cliff. When they reached the top, Captain Donald McDonald of the 78th Highlanders, 'was challenged by a sentry' Knox tells us, 'and with great presence of mind, from his knowledge of French service, answered him according to their manner' telling the sentry that he was coming with a large party to relieve them. It was 0430 hrs and still dark. This gave time for the light infantrymen to make a rush for the guard post. Most of the startled Canadian militiamen were captured, but shots were exchanged and Captain Vergor was wounded. A few militiamen escaped towards the city. The gunfire was heard at the French batteries of Samos and Sillery and by now, it was early dawn. The sentry posts could now see that the supply convoy was in fact a convoy of British boats followed by their warships. The Samos battery opened fire and inflicted some damage and casualties to the British boats and ships. But it was too late. Many soldiers were now forming on the beach under Wolfe's eye and getting up the cliff by the path as fast as they could. The battery was captured at about 0500 hrs by some light infantry. Half an hour later, Wolfe was up to reconnoitre the field. By 0700 hrs, the main body of British troops was moving onto the plains. About an hour later, Burton's and Carleton's men, the last troops to land, were joining the main body on the top of the cliff.

26/6/1759	3/7	10/7	14/7	21/7	28/7	4/8	11/8	18/8	25/8	1/9	8/9	12/9	13/9(0400hrs)	(0700hrs)	(0830hrs)	(1000hrs)	(1130hrs)
pages 65-67 & 68-69			70-74		75-77		78-80						84-91			92-95	

THE HEIGHTS OF ABRAHAM

13th September 1759

The battle

At first, Wolfe formed his men in line facing the Plains of Abraham with their backs to the cliff and Québec City to their right. He must have expected an immediate French attack but nothing came. His good luck continued to hold. There was obviously no important body of French troops yet in the immediate area. The British troops now advanced onto the Plains of Abraham, so named after their original 17th century owner, Abraham Martin. Their line was formed by Wolfe sometime after 0600 hrs with the right being at the cliff. There were initially only three battalions and the Louisbourg Grenadiers, but it extended as more troops came on.

The first line or battle line consisted of the 35th which was next to the cliff and posted a bit farther back. Then came the Louisbourg Grenadiers, the 28th, 43rd, 47th, 78th and the 58th on the left flank. They had to cover a

British troops reach the top of the cliff at Anse-au-Foulon and begin to deploy into line of battle on the Plains of Abraham.
(Print after J. Macfarlane)

26/6/1759	3/7	10/7	14/7	21/7	28/7	4/8	11/8	18/8	25/8	1/9	8/9	12/9	13/9(0400hrs)	(0700hrs)	(0830hrs)	(1000hrs)	(1130hrs)
pages 65-67 & 68-69			70-74		75-77			78-80			81-83						92-95

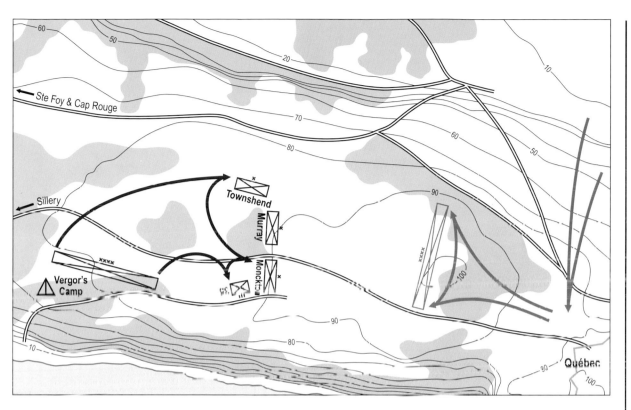

Once Wolfe had formed his army above Anse-au-Foulon he manoeuvred to face toward the city. Meanwhile Montcalm had rushed his forces from the Beauport Lines and assembled them in front of Québec. He then deployed them forward to face the British.

wide area and Wolfe ordered the regiments to align themselves in two ranks instead of the usual three. In the rear of the first line was the 48th forming a very extended second line as a reserve. As Canadian militiamen and Indians appeared on the left of the field skirmishing, Townshend deployed the 15th and the 2nd and 3rd battalions of the 60th to counter them. The 3/60th was later moved back to protect Anse-au-Foulon. To the west of the 58th, the light infantry was deployed near the St Foy road to protect the rear of the British line. Wolfe now had 4,800 men on the Plains, nervous no doubt but pleased to have got this far with no trouble. The weather was cloudy with intermittent rain.

The gunfire from the Samos and Sillery batteries was heard by Montcalm. He thought it was the anticipated supply convoy which had been seen by the British and provoked an exchange of artillery fire. He had been up

all night but, before going to bed, he went to Vaudreuil's HQ to see if there was more information. There he learned from excited officers that the British had managed to land a large force which was deploying on the fields to the west of the city. One of Vergor's men who had escaped had told Lieutenant-Colonel Bernetz, who in turn raced to warn Vaudreuil, the nearest senior commander. It was about 0700 hrs. After a short conversation with Vaudreuil, Montcalm sent his ADC, the Chevalier de Johnstone, to Beauport ordering Lieutenant-Colonel Senezergue to march his brigade of Royal-Roussillon and Guyenne towards the Plains of Abraham. Other couriers rushed off with similar orders for the Trois-Rivières and Québec militias and 600 Montréal militiamen, the battalions of La Sarre, Languedoc and Béarn. Meanwhile, De Répentigny's brigade of militia and colonial troops, posted the closest, had rushed to the Plains before receiving Montcalm's orders. Posted on the side of the Saint-Foy road, they started skirmishing with the British light infantry and Townshend's Brigade (2nd and 3rd battalions 60th and 15th). They were supported by the arrival of the Guyenne and Royal-Roussillon regiments from Beauport.

26/6/1759	3/7	10/7	14/7	21/7	28/7	4/8	11/8	18/8	25/8	1/9	8/9	12/9	13/9(0400hrs)	(0700hrs)	(0830hrs)	(1000hrs)	(1130hrs)
pages 65-67 & 68-69					70-74		75-77		78-80			81-83					92-95

85

General Montcalm at the head of his troops on the Plains of Abraham.
(Print after A.H. Hider. National Archives of Canada, C21457)

Montcalm rode onto the field and must have been astounded by what he saw. Thousands of red-coated soldiers deploying for battle. What could be done now? To wait might mean even more Redcoats. In which case his troops would have to be deployed behind the walls covering the west side of the city. Many in the French camp felt these fortifications to have been totally inadequate and Montcalm was of the same opinion. Thus his motivation to put his men behind the walls would have been very slim. He was a fiery individual and, it should be remembered, a former cavalry officer. The enemy was in front and must be met head on. Exactly what Wolfe was hoping for.

The French regiments arrived and were first posted not very far from the city walls. Eventually, the French positions were as follows: Québec and Trois-Rivières militiamen joined by some Indians, all posted along the Saint-Foy road and already harassing the British left flank. The five French metropolitan battalions were next, deployed from the French right to the left were La Sarre, then Languedoc, Béarn, Guyenne and Royal-Roussillon. This was the main French force which would charge the British. To its left, colonial troops, militiamen and Indians in skirmish order near the edge of the cliff. Nearly all the regular soldiers of the city were on the field but the battalions were nevertheless weak. A few months earlier, some 600 Canadians had been incorporated in their ranks in an effort to boost their numbers. As will be seen later, the French drill sergeants obviously neglected them. But for now, the men were forming up as they prepared, full of nervous hope, to do battle. At most, there could have been around 2,000 metropolitan soldiers plus the 600 Canadians in their ranks and about 1,800 militiamen with some Indians.

Montcalm was among them. Years later, Canadian militiaman Joseph Trahan well recollected 'how Montcalm looked before the engagement. He was riding a dark or black horse in front of our lines, bearing his sword high in the air, in the attitude of encouraging the men to do their duty. He wore a uniform with large sleeves, and the one covering the arm he held in the air, had fallen back, disclosing the white linen of his wristband.'

The formation assumed by the five French regiments as they came onto the battlefield and increasingly close to the British line is the subject of some confusion. Several British officers related that they were advancing in columns, some speak of three columns, while some French officers, notably Malartic, speak of lines. Malartic expressed the opinion that the attack failed because the French did not attack only in columns. There are also accounts that the French line, if it was a line, seemed badly formed – certainly a disadvantage in a battle. Townshend, who later collated information for his reports, mentions that Béarn and Guyenne at the centre were in columns while the units on either side appear to have been in line. It also seemed there was some distance between the three bodies so that it may well have been taken for three columns.

It appears that the explanation might be as follows: to reach the Plains of Abraham, the French troops had to take the road to Sillery. As there was a wood to the right and a bluff to the left, making the advance in line was impossible. The battalions would thus have marched in columns, the Montréal and Trois-Rivières militias and Royal-Roussillon then switching to form a line on the left, the Québec and more Montréal militias with La Sarre and Languedoc striving to do the same on the right. This would be a difficult manoeuvre in an exercise and

26/6/1759 3/7 10/7 14/7 21/7 28/7 4/8 11/8 18/8 25/8 1/9 8/9 12/9 13/9(0400hrs)		(0700hrs) (0830hrs) (1000hrs)	(1130hrs)
pages 65-67 & 68-69	70-74	75-77	78-80	81-83	92-95

performing it while under fire from enemy artillery must have been terribly trying on the good order of the line which was formed. Béarn and Guyenne remained in columns at the centre, the strongest part of the French force. Montcalm must have ordered the manoeuvre of the wings into line for fear of being outflanked. An essential measure, but most unwise for the good formation of the line with companies of men having to run up to about half a kilometre in a matter of minutes. Wolfe had his men already in place, his ground was well covered and his two field guns had opened up. One was placed between the 58th and the 78th, the other between the Louisbourg Grenadiers and the 35th.

The French too had guns but how many is still another matter of debate. The well-known story that the Chevalier de Ramezay commanding in the garrison of Québec had refused 25 field guns to Montcalm turns out to be another fable of the Siege of Québec lore. Apparently taken from Chevalier Johnstone's imaginary *'Dialogue in Hades'* as the authority, Francis Parkman

Montcalm's troops arrived from Beauport to deploy on the Plains. His five army battalions formed line, except for Béarn and Guyenne which remained in column. The militia and colonial troops skirmished on the flanks.

related this in his *'Montcalm and Wolfe'* so convincingly that nearly all historians have since followed it. C.P. Stacey was the notable exception correctly pointing out that there were nowhere near 25 field guns in the city, according to the inventory later taken, and that Ramezay was not present at Québec on 13 September. According to Montbeillard and Foligné, both artillery officers, there were possibly five French guns with Montcalm on the Plains on the flanks of the French line, evidently not very well served.

The intermittent rain had stopped and the cloud cover was clearing. The French troops were moved into position, no doubt exhausted after a rapid march from Beauport. Montbeillard came up to Montcalm who told him that action could not be avoided as the British were entrenching and already had two guns on the field. If he waited, more guns and troops would entrench and it would become impossible to dislodge them 'with the sort of troops we have'. He wondered if Bougainville could hear the gunfire and, looking at the field, he felt 'we were very thin on the ground'. He rode away before Montbeillard could reply.

The skirmishers were having some success firing at the British line and Wolfe ordered his men to lie down until the French regiments advanced. At about 1000 hrs

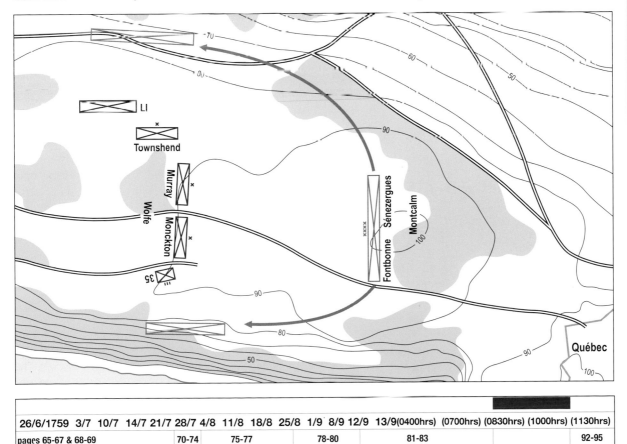

26/6/1759	3/7	10/7	14/7	21/7	28/7	4/8	11/8	18/8	25/8	1/9	8/9	12/9	13/9(0400hrs)	(0700hrs)	(0830hrs)	(1000hrs)	(1130hrs)
pages 65-67 & 68-69			70-74		75-77			78-80			81-83						92-95

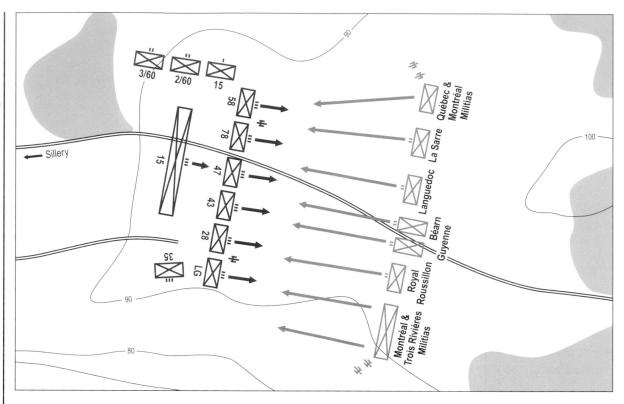

Montcalm gave the order to advance. Wolfe's redcoats stood silent, watching the cheering French approach. They marched much too fast. 'We had not gone twenty steps that the left was too far behind and the centre too much in advance' says Malartic. At about 130 yards, the French line stopped and fired an ineffective volley at the British. True to their long-standing habit, the Canadian militiamen incorporated in the French metropolitan regiments then lay down to reload – one wonders why they had not been drilled to do otherwise. This would not affect firepower very much but added to the disorderly appearance of the French line. It thereafter kept up a sporadic fire as it approached the British although some elements appear to have stayed much further back.

On the British side, Wolfe had given strict orders to his infantry not to open fire until the French were 40 yards away. His two field guns were firing grapeshot into the approaching French. For maximum effect, Wolfe ordered his men to charge their musket with a second ball. The well-disciplined British soldiers stood in their perfect line waiting for the orders to 'present!' and 'fire!'.

'The forty third and the forty-seventh regiments in the center, being little affected by the oblique fire of the

Both armies closed for battle, the French firing an ineffective volley at about 130 yards.

enemy, gave them, with great calmness, as remarkable a close and heavy discharge as I ever saw...' reported Knox who added that 'the French officers say they never opposed such a shock as they received from the centre of our line, for that they believed every ball took place, and such regularity and discipline they had not experienced before; our troops in general, and particularly the central corps, having levelled and fired – comme un coup de canon (like a canon shot).'

This resounding and damaging British volley was not fired by the whole line but only by the 43rd and 47th. Other units opened up a steady platoon fire. The French wavered but kept advancing. The British line then marched ahead a few paces to be clear of the smoke then 'within twenty or thirty yards gave a general' volley says Chief Engineer Mackellar who adds 'upon which a total route of the Enemy immediately ensued.' Montbeillard noted however that 'rout was total only among the regular (metropolitan) troops. The Canadians who were accustomed to withdraw and then come back to (engage) the enemy with more resolve than

26/6/1759	3/7	10/7	14/7	21/7	28/7	4/8	11/8	18/8	25/8	1/9	8/9	12/9	13/9(0400hrs)	(0700hrs)	(0830hrs)	(1000hrs)	(1130hrs)
pages 65-67 & 68-69			70-74		75-77			78-80			81-83						92-95

**The battle on the Plains of Abraham,
13 September 1759.**
(Print after George Campion, C,1850 (National Archives of
Canada, C4501)

previously, rallied in several places.' Later events proved
Montebeillard's observations to be correct.

However, the French were still firing at the British,
especially the Canadian militiamen skirmishing on the
flanks, and at about this time, Wolfe, who was charging
with the Louisbourg Grenadiers and the 28th, was hit.
He 'first received a musket ball thro' his right wrist, but
he wrapped his handkerchief round it, and marched on.

**At a range of 40 yards the British delivered the first of
two devastating volleys which broke the French line.**

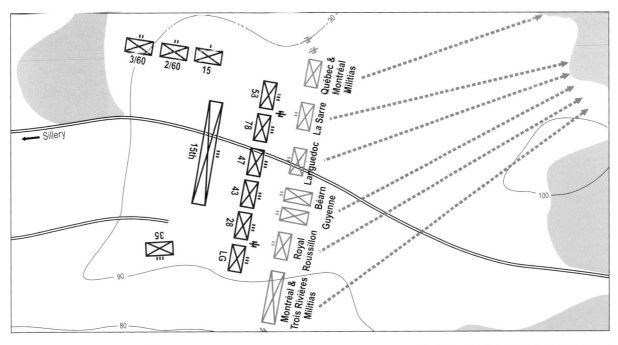

26/6/1759	3/7	10/7	14/7	21/7	28/7	4/8	11/8	18/8	25/8	1/9	8/9	12/9	13/9(0400hrs)	(0700hrs)	(0830hrs)	(1000hrs)	(1130hrs)
pages 65-67 & 68-69			70-74		75-77		78-80			81-83						92-95	

The next he received was in his belly, about an inch below the navel, and the third shot just above the breast' later reported an anonymous witness to the Gentleman's Magazine. Again, there are a good many stories as to who shot Wolfe but the most likely cause of his death remains an unknown Canadian or colonial soldier firing from the bushes near the cliff.

Of all the accounts of Wolfe's last moments, John Knox's remains the one generally accepted as the most credible. After Wolfe was 'carried off wounded to the rear of the front line, he desired those who were about him to lay him down; being asked if he would have a surgeon, he replied, "it is needless, it is all over with me." One of them cried then out, "they run, see how they run". "Who runs?" demanded our hero, with great earnestness, like a person roused from sleep. The officer answered, "the enemy, Sir; egad, they give way everywhere". Thereupon the general rejoined, "Go one of you, my lads, to Colonel Burton – ; tell him to march Webb's regiment with all speed down to Charles's river,

The British infantry go in with the bayonet.
(National Archives of Canada, C20756)

to cut off the retreat of the fugitives of the bridge". Turning on his side, he added, "Now, God be praised, I will die in peace": and thus expired.'

A pair of flint-lock pistols belonging to General Wolfe.

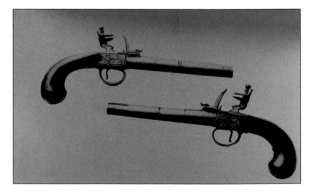

26/6/1759	3/7	10/7	14/7	21/7	28/7	4/8	11/8	18/8	25/8	1/9	8/9	12/9	13/9(0400hrs)	(0700hrs)	(0830hrs)	(1000hrs)	(1130hrs)
pages 65-67 & 68-69			70-74		75-77			78-80			81-83						92-95

The death of General Wolfe was probably the closest to something like this representation. Of the various accounts of his last moments, the most plausible version appears to be Captain Knox's account which mentions only Lieutenant Browne, a volunteer and a grenadier, all of the Louisbourg Grenadiers.
(Print after Edward Penney's 1764 painting)

Knox went on to state that 'Various accounts have been circulated of General Wolfe's manner of dying, his last words, and the officers into whose hands he fell: and many, from a vanity of talking, claimed the honour of being his supporters after he was wounded; but the foregoing circumstances were ascertained to me by Lieutenant Brown, of the grenadiers of Louisbourg and the twenty-second regiment, who, with Mr. Henderson, a volunteer in the same company, and a private man, were the three persons who carried his excellency to the rear; which an artillery officer seeing, immediately flew to his assistance; and these were all that attended him in his dying moments.'

It may have been at about this time that Montcalm was hit, possibly while trying to rally some of his soldiers. Militiaman Trahan, who seems to have been one of those drafted into a French metropolitan battalion, recalled that 'when he (Montcalm) was

wounded, a rumour spread that he was killed; a panic ensued...' As with his opponent, there are several versions of what happened. Williamson of the Royal Artillery claimed grape shot from one of his six-pounders hit the French general. It could have been repeated musket fire too as he made a fine target mounted on his horse. In any event the multiple wounds, in the lower stomach and the thigh, were quite serious. Three soldiers helped support him on his horse as he came back into the city.

Besides Montcalm, the French suffered simultaneously several serious losses to its senior officers which had a destabilising effect. The second in command, Brigadier de Sénézergue was hit and badly wounded, as was Lieutenant-Colonel de Fontbrune. According to Major Malartic, whose horse was shot from under him, La Sarre and Guyenne suffered the most casualties.

Badly wounded, General Montcalm is helped back into Québec. (Print after Louis Bombled)

26/6/1759	3/7	10/7	14/7	21/7	28/7	4/8	11/8	18/8	25/8	1/9	8/9	12/9	13/9(0400hrs)	(0700hrs)	(0830hrs)	(1000hrs)	(1130hrs)
pages 65-67 & 68-69			70-74		75-77			78-80			81-83					92-95	

THE HEIGHTS OF ABRAHAM

Finale

It was during the British charges in pursuit of the French that they suffered the most casualties. No doubt, a number of Louisbourg Grenadiers and men of the 28th were hit. Some of the senior British officers were wounded in the engagement as well, Monckton badly and Carleton was hit in the head. Barré too was hit. Brigadier Murray directed Fraser's 78th Highlanders to charge the French right. The highlanders came out wielding their broadswords and the French fled. It was at this point that the French side could be said to have split in two. On one hand, there were the French metropolitan soldiers, panic stricken who kept running into the city or all the way to Beauport. On the other, the Canadian militiamen who rallied and fought on fiercely.

'I can remember the Scotch Highlanders flying wildly after us, with streaming plaid, bonnets and large swords – like so many infuriated demons, over the brow of the hill' said militiaman Trahan. However, things were about to change as they neared a wooded area. 'In their course was a wood, in which we had some Indians and sharpshooters, who bowled over the Sauvages d'Écosse (Scottish Savages) in fine style. Their partly naked bodies fell on their face, and their kilts in disorder

French officers try to rally the rout of their troops at the Plains of Abraham. The dress of the French troops is not accurately rendered.
(Print after J. Macfarlane)

26/6/1759	3/7	10/7	14/7	21/7	28/7	4/8	11/8	18/8	25/8	1/9	8/9	12/9	13/9(0400hrs)	(0700hrs)	(0830hrs)	(1000hrs)	(1130hrs)
pages 65-67 & 68-69			70-74		75-77			78-80			81-83				84-91		

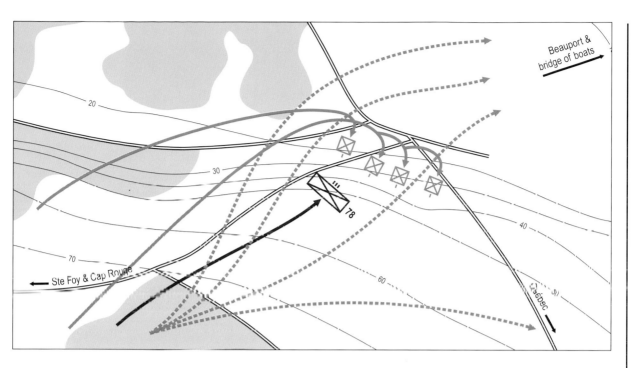

Beauport &
bridge of boats

Ste Foy & Cap Rouge

The final phase of the battle of the Heights of Abraham. The British regiments had broken out in pursuit of the fleeing French. Fraser's 78th Foot faced stiff resistance by Canadian militiamen covering the retreat in the woods.

left exposed a portion of their thighs, at which our fugitives passing by, would make lunges with their swords, cutting large slices out of the fleshiest portion of their persons.' There seem to have been few Indians but there certainly were several hundred Canadian militiamen who were now fighting in their own style. They were so effective that, reported Lieutenant Fraser, 'they killed a great many of our men, and killed two Officers, which obliged us to retire a little, and form again'. Murray now directed Anstruther's 58th and the 2nd battalion of the 60th Royal Americans to rescue the 78th Highlanders and clear the woods so victory could be complete. The Canadian militiamen were now outnumbered and finally gave way, fighting as they retreated.

The battle was ending as Vaudreuil arrived from Beauport. He had been rallying up to about a thousand Canadian militiamen and sent them ahead with all speed under Dumas. These were essentially the troops that the 78th Highlanders ran into and who covered the French retreat.

On the west side of the Plain, at about 1100 hrs, elements of Bougainville's Corps came into sight and 'formed in a line as if he intended to attack us' recalled Fraser. Townshend directed the light infantry, the 48th and the 3/60th with some field piece towards them. A few shots were fired and Bougainville's force began to withdraw.

In all, the British had 61 killed and 603 wounded (Townshend reported 58 killed and 600 wounded). Fraser's 78th Highlanders suffered the most with 18 killed and 148 wounded followed by the 60th Royal Americans with 98 casualties and Anstruther's 58th with 97. Most of the casualties were sustained in the skirmishing before and after the main battle.

The French casualties were reported at about 640 killed, wounded and missing by Vaudreuil, a figure which seems low. Montbeillard estimated between 700 and 800. La Pause left a more detailed account for metropolitan and colonial troops which mentioned 150 killed including 13 officers, 370 made prisoner including 18 officers and 28 missing. The number of wounded is not given but 193 died of their wounds in the General Hospital. And this does not include the casualties of the militia companies although 110 were captured. All in all, French casualties and prisoners may have been between 900 and 1,000. Among the senior officers killed were Senezergue and Fontbrune, the next after

26/6/1759	3/7	10/7	14/7	21/7	28/7	4/8	11/8	18/8	25/8	1/9	8/9	12/9	13/9(0400hrs)	(0700hrs)	(0830hrs)	(1000hrs)	(1130hrs)
pages 65-67 & 68-69			70-74		75-77		78-80			81-83			84-91				

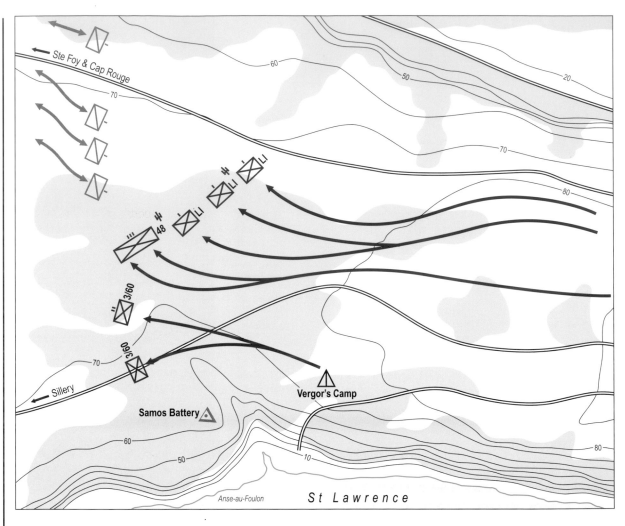

Ste Foy & Cap Rouge

Sillery

Samos Battery

Vergor's Camp

Anse-au-Foulon

St Lawrence

Part of the British forces, including the 3/60th who had earlier been detailed to guard the landing site, turned to face Bougainville's forces arriving from the west.

Montcalm in seniority.

Montcalm was badly wounded and had been seen by many people entering the city. He was taken to surgeon Arnoux's house and once he had seen his wounds, Montcalm asked him to tell him 'the truth like a sincere friend.' The surgeon told him he would die before the morning at which Montcalm replied 'Good, I will not see the English in Québec.' He died at 0500 hrs on the 14th and was put in a makeshift coffin and, after a short service, buried in large crater made by a British bomb in the floor of the Ursuline sisters chapel.

Vaudreuil had convened a war council in the afternoon of the 13th to propose a renewed attack the next day. Intendant Bigot strongly supported the idea but all the other officers, discouraged, rejected the plan. That night, the French forces evacuated their positions at Beauport and marched to the west of the city towards Lorette. Many militiamen deserted and went back to their homes during the night. The garrison left in Québec was in an impossible situation. They were mostly militiamen and sailors with fewer than 200 regulars and had little food and ammunition. On the 15th, they petitioned Sieur de Ramezay, the remaining senior officer, to surrender. Only colonial artillery officer Jacau de Fiedmont wished to fight to the last. Faced with this, Ramezay sought to obtain as honourable acapitulation as possible from Townshend.

On the 17th, General Lévis arrived in the Québec area and assumed command of the troops such as they were. Bougainville had rallied, as best he could, the

26/6/1759	3/7	10/7	14/7	21/7	28/7	4/8	11/8	18/8	25/8	1/9	8/9	12/9	13/9(0400hrs)	(0700hrs)	(0830hrs)	(1000hrs)	(1130hrs)
pages 65-67 & 68-69			70-74		75-77		78-80		81-83				84-91				

Death of General Montcalm in 1759, an imaginary scene in a print after Desfontaines, c. 1792.
(National Archives of Canada, C3702)

remnants of the battalions. Lévis' arrival raised their morale and he told them the city could still be saved if reinforcements could be brought in. Bougainville with a few elite troops was sent ahead to try to get into the city.

Meanwhile, de Ramezay's situation was just about untenable and he wished to avoid a general assault on the city. Negotiations for surrender had started on the 17th. Inside the city, the spirit of the defenders was very

John Hale, here in the uniform of the 17th Light Dragoons, was sent to London to announce the fall of Québec.
(After a portrait c. 1765 by Sir Joshua Reynolds. National Archives of Canada C4663)

low. According to Town Major de Joannès who was Ramezay's second-in-command, many were close to mutiny and desertion if asked to make a further stand. Wrote de Joannès: 'It is true that most of the militiamen and the sailors composing the garrison of Québec were of the worst bad will. The bad comments made by the officer of these troops had angered me to the point of striking two of these officers with my sword. They threatened nothing less than abandoning their posts and having their troops abandon them too. One can see from this their bad dispositions. Several had even escaped and deserted.'

This, and other similar reports, must have had a profound effect on de Ramezay. He doubted the capacity of Lévis' and Bougainville's troops to beat the British army now before the gates of the city. Although later blamed for not defending the city in a siege because his experience was in wilderness warfare, de Ramezay believed that his discouraged and mutinous irregular troops could never stand an assault by the seasoned British regulars. A sustained general assault by the British grenadiers would have surely slaughtered the militiamen and could well have deteriorated into a general and unbridled carnage on the civilians in the city. With all this in mind, de Ramezay agreed to Québec's capitulation late on the evening of the 17th if help had not arrived by 2300 hrs. Town Major Joannès then went to Townshend with the news.

About half an hour later, Captain de la Roche Beaucourt with 60 troopers of the Corps of Cavalry rode into the city promising help. But it was all too late and it is doubtful how much help could really have been given to the mutinous militia garrison, certainly unsuited for intense siege warfare even if it had been in great spirits. And Townshend's thousands of redcoats would first have to be defeated – a proposition next to impossible considering the disorganisation and dispersal of the French forces. Accordingly, de Ramezay signed the capitulation on 18 September. It granted the Honours of War to the French garrison and the repatriation to France of the ten officers and 172 soldiers belonging to the metropolitan regiments.

For Lévis, there was nothing further he could do. But Montcalm's army was not destroyed. It had now regrouped under Lévis, certainly the most able of the French senior commanders. It was not over. They would return to Montréal and reorganise. They would gain strength. Encouraged, they would be back in the spring...

26/6/1759	3/7	10/7	14/7	21/7	28/7	4/8	11/8	18/8	25/8	1/9	8/9	12/9	13/9(0400hrs)	(0700hrs)	(0830hrs)	(1000hrs)	(1130hrs)
pages 65-67 & 68-69			70-74		75-77		78-80			81-83			84-91				

WARGAMING QUÉBEC

If Louisbourg was the key to Québec, then Québec was the key to New France. The historical result of the Battle of the Heights of Abraham (or the Battle of the Plains) in 1759 effectively lost the French their possessions in New France and promoted Britain, for a short time, to undisputed colonial master of North America.

Given free play, what would happen if the grenadiers succeeded in scaling the cliffs at Montmorency or if stiff opposition had been encountered at the Anse-au-Foulon. Alternatively, were the two French metropolitan regiments, Guyenne and Béarn, deliberately deployed in column, in the manner of the Chevalier de Folard's two-battalion column 'l'ordre profond', or did they just not have time to change from column of march into line on arrival from Beauport. The player representing Montcalm might deploy all his metropolitan regiments in two such 'shock action' columns and attack.

Another interesting scenario which can be played is if Montcalm holds his position in front of Québec City and awaits the arrival of Bougainville from Cap Rouge, thus catching the British between his two forces.

Québec offers the wargamer the rare opportunity of mixing tactics. There is the formal set-piece European warfare of the mid-18th century as exemplified by the Battle of the Plains. And there is the opportunity to fight any number of small engagements between the British and the Canadian militias and Indians, practising their 'irregular' warfare.

SELECT BIBLIOGRAPHY

Manuscript sources

Archives de la Guerre, series A1, Vol. 3540 and 3541 at the Service Historique de l'Armée de Terre in Vincennes, France. Archives Nationales (France), Colonies, series B, Vols. 109 and 110 and C11A, Vol. 104 and series K, Monuments Historiques, carton 1232. Northcliffe Collection, National Archives of Canada, MG 18, K and M. Possibly the most outstanding collection anywhere concerning the Quebec campaign.

Publications

Bougainville, Louis-Antoine de. *Adventure in the Wildeness: the American Journals of Louis Antoine de Bougainville 1756-1760* ed. & transl. by Edward P. Hamilton (Norman, University of Oklahoma, 1964).

Deschênes, Gaston. *L'Année des Anglais: la Côte-du-Sud à l'heure de la Conquête* (Sillery [Québec], Septentrion, 1988).

Dictionary of Canadian Biography (Toronto and Québec City, University of Toronto & Université Laval, 1974-1983), Vols. 3-5.

Doughty, Sir Arthur, with A.G. Palmette. *The Siege of Quebec and the Battle of the Plains of Abraham* (6 Vols., Quebec, 1901).

Filteau, Gérard. *Par la bouche de mes canons: la ville de Québec face à l'ennemi* (Sillery [Québec], Septentrion, 1990)

Hébert, Jean-Claude, ed. *Le siége de Québec en 1759 par trois témoins* (Québec, Ministère des Affaires culturelles, 1972).

Knox, John. *An Historical Journal of the Campaigns in North America* (London, 1769 and many reprints and editions since).

Malartic, Comte de Maurés de. *Journal des Campagnes au Canada de 1755 à 1760* (Paris, 1890).

Stacey, C.P. *Quebec, 1759: The Siege and the Battle* (Toronto, Macmillan, 1959) and *Quebec, 1759: Some New Documents*, The Canadian Historical Review, XLVII, No. 4, Dec., 1966.